BREADS

D0953610

by
Jean Paré

Dedication

The greatest thing! It's *still* sliced bread!

Cover Photo

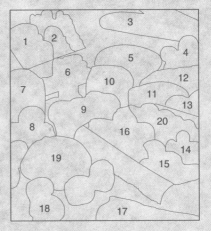

Cabinet Courtesy Of:
Chintz & Company

Table Courtesy Of:
Sissy Walker's Country Interiors

BREADS

Third Printing December 1996

ISBN 1-895455-09-X

Published and Distributed by
Company's Coming Publishing Limited
Box 8037, Station "F"
Edmonton, Alberta, Canada
T6H 4N9

**Published Simultaneously in
Canada and the United States of America**

Printed In Canada

Company's Coming Cookbooks
by Jean Paré

table of Contents

Jean Paré grew up understanding that the combination of family, friends and home cooking is the essence of a good life. From her mother she learned to appreciate good cooking, while her father praised even her earliest attempts. When she left home she took with her many acquired family recipes, her love of cooking and her intriguing desire to read recipe books like novels!

In 1963, when her four children had all reached school age, Jean volunteered to cater to the 50th anniversary of the Vermilion School of Agriculture, now Lakeland College. Working out of her home, Jean prepared a dinner for over 1000 people which launched a flourishing catering operation that continued for over eighteen years. During that time she was provided with countless opportunities to test new ideas with immediate feedback—resulting in empty plates and contented customers! Whether preparing cocktail sandwiches for a house party or serving a hot meal for 1500 people, Jean Paré earned a reputation for good food, courteous service and reasonable prices.

"Why don't you write a cookbook?" Time and again, as requests for her recipes mounted, Jean was asked that question. Jean's response was to team up with her son, Grant Lovig, in the fall of 1980 to form Company's Coming Publishing Limited. April 14, 1981, marked the debut of "150 DELICIOUS SQUARES", the first Company's Coming cookbook in what soon would become Canada's most popular cookbook series. By 1995, sales had surpassed ten million cookbooks.

Jean Paré's operation has grown from the early days of working out of a spare bedroom in her home to operating a large and fully equipped test kitchen in Vermilion, Alberta, near the home she and her husband Larry built. Full-time staff has grown steadily to include marketing personnel located in major cities across Canada plus selected U.S. markets. Home Office is located in Edmonton, Alberta where distribution, accounting and administration functions are headquartered in the company's own 20,000 square foot facility. Growth continues with the recent addition of the Recipe Factory, a 2700 square foot test kitchen and photography studio located in Edmonton.

Company's Coming cookbooks are now distributed throughout Canada and the United States plus numerous overseas markets, all under the guidance of Jean's daughter, Gail Lovig. The series is published in English and French, plus a Spanish language edition is available in Mexico. Soon the familiar and trusted Company's Coming style of recipes will be available in a variety of formats in addition to the bestselling soft cover series.

Jean Paré's approach to cooking has always called for quick and easy recipes using everyday ingredients. She continues to gain new supporters by adhering to what she calls "the golden rule of cooking": never share a recipe you wouldn't use yourself. It's an approach that works—*ten million times over!*

Bread, the staff of life. Throughout the ages, bread has been considered the most basic and fundamental of foods. In today's world of hustle and bustle, there are many who see breadmaking as a complicated and difficult art best left to the experienced chef. But there really is no mystery surrounding this age-old tradition. Bread is created from flour, yeast, salt and water, with added ingredients such as sugar, eggs and milk to create flavor and texture. In modern times, we benefit from the use of instant yeast, which shortens the time needed to allow the dough to rise.

No one has an inborn knack for baking good bread. Like many things in life, it comes with the doing. After just a little practice you will learn to know when the dough feels right—gummy, elastic and shiny. And even while you experiment, each and every loaf you make is wonderful to eat fresh and warm. Most bread recipes make two loaves, and all recipes make manageable amounts. Mixing and kneading the dough goes fairly quickly, however attention should be given to the rising dough. Plan to allow enough time. It's a good opportunity to get some other things done while waiting. Should you find it becomes necessary to leave for a short time, simply punch your dough down and refrigerate it until your return.

We all have our daily bread, so we should add variety. Anadama Bread is sure to become a family favorite, as will Seedy Rolls. How about Sticky Cinnamon Buns? Don't forget Sugared Doughnuts for a delicious after-school treat. Apple Kuchen is perfect whether it's for morning coffee, afternoon tea or evening dessert. If you own a bread machine, you will be pleased to know that several recipes have been included specifically for bread machines.

Bread is usually best fresh from the oven. And that aroma—heavenly! Fresh or not, toasted bread is high on anyone's list of comfort foods. So whether expecting company or feeding the family, bake a little goodness into your next meal. Bring on the bread!

Jean Paré

Glossary

Baking and Cooling: Yeast breads bake in less time than quick breads. When the bottom of a loaf is tapped it will sound hollow when done. Tapping a loaf on top will also sound hollow. It is more difficult to hear a hollow sound when tapping heavy, dense bread. It is a good rule to time your loaves and jot it down for next time. An instant-read thermometer will show 200°F (93°C) when done. Remove from pans to racks quickly to avoid sogginess.

Batter Breads: Ingredients are mixed together. Batter is too soft to knead. Usually one rising is all that is required. The crumb is more open-textured than kneaded bread. Very easy to make.

Bread Machine Bread: These require the least amount of work. A good idea to save even more time is to make up several bags, each containing all of the dry ingredients (except yeast) used for your favorite loaf. Simply pour in wet ingredients, then the dry, then the yeast. Let the machine take over. The bread machine recipes in this book were tested in a Regal Kitchen Pro bread machine that makes 1 to 2 lb. (500 g to 1 kg) loaves.

Crusts and Glazes:

a) Before baking, brush tops with milk. It adds color and a tender crust.

b) Before baking, beat 1 egg white and 1 tbsp. (15 mL) water with fork. Brush tops. It will give bread a crisp crust. It will also help seeds to stick. It gives some shine to the tops.

c) Before baking, brush tops with water. It gives bread a crisp crust. It helps even more to spray with water one or more times during baking.

d) After baking, brush hot tops with softened butter or margarine. Crust will be shiny and soft.

e) To increase crust, remove bread from pans during the last five minutes of baking and place directly on oven racks to finish baking.

f) Before baking, beat one egg yolk and 2 tsp. (10 mL) water with fork. Brush tops. It will give a rich brown color. This may be done 10 minutes before removing from the oven if tops are not brown enough.

g) Loaves brushed with a beaten egg or egg white will hold seeds.

h) After baking, brush hot tops with 1 tbsp. (15 mL) granulated sugar dissolved in same amount of water. Crust will be crisp.

i) Do nothing and you will have a crispy crust.

(continued on next page)

Dough: First the yeast is dissolved, then mixed with all ingredients. It is kneaded 8 to 10 minutes until smooth, shiny and elastic. It is covered and allowed to rise, punched down, panned and allowed to rise a second time before baking. Using instant yeast cuts down on the rising time.

Eggs: Add nutrition and color, providing for a richer product.

Fat: Whether you use butter, margarine, cooking oil, shortening or lard it will give a more tender and moist product. It also improves keeping qualities.

Flour: Wheat flour (all-purpose) contains hard wheat which contains gluten. This helps to hold the gas bubbles formed by the yeast which results in a lighter product.

Freezing: All bread recipes in this book can be frozen. Cool thoroughly. Freeze in moisture-proof bags. Thaw while wrapped. For warm, freshened bread, wrap in foil and heat in 350°F (175°C) oven for 10 minutes or until warm.

Heavy Mixer: Unless you enjoy the kneading part of breadmaking this is a wonderful kitchen appliance. About two minutes of machine kneading is equal to 8 to 10 minutes of kneading by hand. This is a must for arthritic cooks.

Kneading: To knead dough by hand, place ball of dough on lightly floured surface. Dust your hands with flour. Push dough down to flatten a bit. Fold dough over towards you. Using the heels of your hands push down and away from you. Repeat five or six times. Give dough a quarter turn. Repeat. Use flour as needed if dough becomes sticky. You will know it has been kneaded long enough. It will be smooth and elastic (gummy). When you press dough with your finger, it will spring back. To knead by machine, follow machine's directions. Either way the resulting satiny mixture will produce nicely-textured bread and buns, although you will probably bake more often if you have a strong mixer.

Liquid Temperature: 100°F (38°C) is best for dissolving yeast granules, 80°F (27°C) for fresh yeast. 100°F (38°C) will feel nice and warm if you touch it with the inner side of your wrist. Hot water kills yeast. Take into consideration your bowl temperature. If for example you use a large cold bowl to dissolve yeast, the warm water will cool immediately, slowing yeast action.

(continued on next page)

Mixing: After adding as much flour as the beater can handle, begin to mix in additional flour with a spoon. As dough is worked it will pull away from the sides of the bowl. If it is too difficult to work by hand, turn the dough onto a lightly floured surface. Work additional flour into the dough as you knead it. Remember, less is best. As the dough begins to lose its stickiness, add flour about 1 tbsp. (15 mL) at a time.

Risen Enough: When dough appears to have doubled in bulk, poke 2 finger-tips into it. If the imprint remains, the dough has risen sufficiently. When testing the dough after it has risen in pans, carefully poke one fingertip in the end, not too far. Dent should remain. Touched lightly, the dough will feel full of air. Remove pans from oven to counter while oven reaches baking temperature. Remove cover and bake.

Rising: A warm, draft-free place is important. Turn the oven on to the lowest setting for 30 seconds. Turn off heat. Turn oven light on. Place covered bowl of dough in oven. Close oven door. Dough will rise undisturbed.

Salt: Salt acts as a control for yeast action. It also adds greatly to the flavor.

Shaping: An egg-sized bun is a medium bun. If you have a scale, each piece of dough should weigh 2 oz. (56 g). Using a scale is a sure way to get evenly-sized buns. Flatten the piece of dough, draw all the edges together and place seam-side down on a greased pan. This will create a smooth, rounded top. To make hamburger buns, use dough the size of a tennis ball, 4 oz. (112 g). If you want buns with soft sides, place ½ inch (12 mm) apart. For separated buns place 2 to 2½ inches (5 to 6 cm) apart. Bread may be simply shaped into a loaf and placed in pan. It may also be rolled out into a rectangle, rolled up from one end like a jelly roll and placed in pan. This method lends itself to sprinkling with cinnamon and raisins or any other flavor before rolling.

Sponge: Yeast is dissolved and mixed with sugar and part of the flour. It is allowed to rise until bubbly and spongy-looking. The remaining ingredients are mixed in, then kneaded. There are 2 risings before baking.

Sugar: Sugar acts as food for the yeast. It helps produce carbon dioxide. Sugar is also added for flavor, and helps browning. Honey and molasses may also be used to add flavor.

Water/Milk/Juices: Liquids bind ingredients. Water gives a crispier crust. Milk gives a softer crumb. Milk is usually scalded and cooled although with pasteurization it is not always done but rather just warmed.

Yeast: Active dry yeast and instant yeast (fast-rising or quick-rising) are granular and packaged in ¼ oz. (8 g) envelopes or in bulk containers. One level tablespoon (15 mL) of bulk yeast is equivalent to one envelope of packaged yeast. Active dry or instant yeast keeps longer than fresh yeast cakes and may be interchanged. Active dry yeast is dissolved in a mixture of sugar and warm water. Instant yeast is simply added to the dry ingredients and is not dissolved before using. A cake of yeast does not require sugar when dissolving in 80°F (27°C) liquid.

A good nutty taste. Quite a coarse texture.

Warm water	1¼ cups	300 mL
Granulated sugar	1 tsp.	5 mL
Active dry yeast	1 × ¼ oz.	1 × 8 g
Milk, scalded and cooled to lukewarm	1 cup	250 mL
Quick rolled oats	¼ cup	60 mL
Natural bran (not cereal)	¼ cup	60 mL
Wheat germ	¼ cup	60 mL
Mild molasses	3 tbsp.	50 mL
Butter or hard margarine, softened	2 tbsp.	30 mL
Salt	2 tsp.	10 mL
Large egg	1	1
Whole wheat flour	2 cups	500 mL
Sunflower seeds (or sesame seeds)	¼ cup	60 mL
All-purpose flour	1 cup	250 mL
All-purpose flour	1½ cups	375 mL
Butter or hard margarine, softened, for brushing tops	2 tsp.	10 mL

Stir sugar in warm water in small bowl. Sprinkle yeast over top. Let stand 10 minutes. Stir to dissolve yeast.

Combine next 8 ingredients in large bowl. Beat. Add yeast mixture. Beat well.

Beat in whole wheat flour. Add sunflower seeds and first amount of all-purpose flour. Beat in. Cover with greased waxed paper and tea towel. Let stand in oven with light on and door closed for about 45 minutes until doubled in bulk. Stir batter down.

Add remaining flour. Mix well. Spoon into 2 greased 9 × 5 × 3 inch (22 × 12 × 7 cm) loaf pans. Cover with greased waxed paper and tea towel. Let stand in oven with light on and door closed for about 1 hour until doubled in size. Bake in 350°F (175°C) oven for about 30 minutes. Turn out onto racks to cool.

Brush warm tops with second amount of butter. Makes 2 loaves.

Pictured on page 17.

OATMEAL BATTER BREAD

A light and flavorful loaf.

Rolled oats (not instant)	⅔ cup	150 mL
Boiling water	1¼ cups	300 mL
Mild molasses	¼ cup	60 mL
Butter or hard margarine	2 tbsp.	30 mL
Salt	1 tsp.	5 mL
Granulated sugar	1 tsp.	5 mL
Warm water	¼ cup	60 mL
Active dry yeast	1 x ¼ oz.	1 x 8 g
Large egg	1	1
All-purpose flour	3 cups	750 mL
Butter or hard margarine, softened, for brushing tops	2 tsp.	10 mL

Measure rolled oats into large bowl. Pour boiling water over oats. Stir.

Add molasses, first amount of butter and salt. Stir well. Cool to lukewarm.

Stir sugar in warm water in small bowl. Sprinkle yeast over top. Let stand 10 minutes. Stir to dissolve yeast. Add to oat mixture.

Beat in egg. Beat in flour. Cover with greased waxed paper and tea towel. Let stand in oven with light on and door closed for about 1 hour until doubled in bulk. Stir batter down. Spoon into 2 greased 8 x 4 inch (20 x 10 cm) loaf pans. Cover with greased waxed paper and tea towel. Let stand in oven with light on and door closed for 35 to 45 minutes until doubled in size. Bake in 375°F (190°C) oven for about 35 minutes. Turn out onto racks to cool.

Brush warm tops with second amount of butter. Makes 2 loaves.

Pictured on page 17.

There's a fortune to be made in making marbles. So many people seem to have lost theirs.

A good, easy bread. Dense in texture.

Granulated sugar	1 tsp.	5 mL
Warm water	¼ cup	60 mL
Active dry yeast	1 x ¼ oz.	1 x 8 g
Milk, scalded and cooled to lukewarm	1 cup	250 mL
Brown sugar, packed	3 tbsp.	50 mL
Butter or hard margarine, softened	3 tbsp.	50 mL
Salt	1½ tsp.	7 mL
All-purpose flour	1½ cups	375 mL
Rye flour	1 cup	250 mL
All-purpose flour	½ cup	125 mL
Butter or hard margarine, softened, for brushing tops	1 tsp.	5 mL

Stir first amount of sugar in warm water in small bowl. Sprinkle yeast over top. Let stand 10 minutes. Stir to dissolve yeast.

Combine milk, brown sugar, first amount of butter and salt in large bowl. Add yeast mixture. Stir.

Add first amount of flour. Beat on low to moisten. Beat on medium for about 2 minutes until smooth.

Add rye flour and remaining all-purpose flour. Beat well. Cover with greased waxed paper and tea towel. Let stand in oven with light on and door closed for about 1 hour until doubled in bulk. Work batter down. Turn into greased 1½ quart (1.5 L) casserole. Cover with greased waxed paper and tea towel. Let stand for 30 minutes in oven with light on and door closed until doubled in size. Bake in 375°F (190°C) oven for about 30 minutes. Turn out onto rack to cool.

Brush warm tops with second amount of butter. Cut into wedges. Serve warm or cold. Makes 1 loaf.

Pictured on page 17.

BROWN BATTER BREAD

A golden color with flavor to match.

Granulated sugar	2 tsp.	10 mL
Warm water	½ cup	125 mL
Active dry yeast	1 × ¼ oz.	1 × 8 g
Milk	1¼ cups	300 mL
Molasses, mild or dark	¼ cup	60 mL
Granulated sugar	¼ cup	60 mL
Butter or hard margarine	½ cup	125 mL
Salt	2 tsp.	10 mL
Large eggs	2	2
Whole wheat flour	2½ cups	625 mL
All-purpose flour	3 cups	750 mL
Butter or hard margarine, softened, for brushing tops	2 tsp.	10 mL

Stir first amount of sugar in warm water in small bowl. Sprinkle yeast over top. Let stand 10 minutes. Stir to dissolve yeast.

Scald milk in saucepan. Remove from heat. Add next 4 ingredients. Stir until sugar is dissolved and butter is melted. Cool to lukewarm. Add yeast mixture. Pour into large bowl.

Beat in eggs. Gradually beat in both flours. Cover with greased waxed paper and tea towel. Let stand in oven with light on and door closed for about 1¼ hours until doubled in bulk. Stir batter down. Divide dough between 2 greased 9 × 5 × 3 inch (22 × 12 × 7 cm) loaf pans. Cover with greased waxed paper and tea towel. Let stand in oven with light on and door closed for about 1 hour until doubled in size. Bake in 375°F (190°C) oven for 30 to 35 minutes. Turn out onto racks to cool.

Brush warm tops with second amount of butter. Makes 2 loaves.

Pictured on page 17.

Paré Pointer

A sandwich is really a witch that lives by the sea.

A large loaf. Fine-textured and a yellowish color. Good flavor.

Yellow cornmeal	½ cup	125 mL
Boiling water	1 cup	250 mL
Butter or hard margarine	2 tbsp.	30 mL
Mild molasses	¼ cup	60 mL
Salt	1 tsp.	5 mL
Granulated sugar	1 tsp.	5 mL
Warm water	¼ cup	60 mL
Active dry yeast	1 x ¼ oz.	1 x 8 g
Large egg	1	1
All-purpose flour	2¾ cups	675 mL
Butter or hard margarine, softened, for brushing top	1 tsp.	5 mL

Measure cornmeal into large bowl. Add boiling water. Stir.

Add next 3 ingredients. Stir to melt butter. Cool to lukewarm.

Stir sugar in warm water in small bowl. Sprinkle yeast over top. Let stand 10 minutes. Stir to dissolve yeast. Add to cornmeal mixture. Stir.

Beat in egg. Beat in flour gradually. Cover with greased waxed paper and tea towel. Let stand in oven with light on and door closed for about 1¼ hours until doubled in bulk. Stir batter down. Place in greased 9 x 5 x 3 inch (22 x 12 x 7 cm) loaf pan. Cover with greased waxed paper and tea towel. Let stand in oven with light on and door closed for about 45 minutes until doubled in size. Bake in 375°F (190°C) oven for 30 to 35 minutes. Turn out onto rack to cool.

Brush warm top with butter. Makes 1 loaf.

At the end of an athlete's leg do you find athlete's foot?

WHOLE WHEAT BATTER BREAD

This tasty dense loaf is quick and easy. No kneading or rising time and it is 100% whole wheat.

Granulated sugar	1 tsp.	5 mL
Warm water	½ cup	125 mL
Active dry yeast	1 × ¼ oz.	1 × 8 g
Whole wheat flour	4 cups	1 L
Brown sugar, packed	1 tbsp.	15 mL
Salt	1 tsp.	5 mL
Natural bran (not cereal)	¼ cup	60 mL
Wheat germ, toasted	¼ cup	60 mL
Warm water	1½ cups	375 mL
Cooking oil	¼ cup	60 mL
Butter or hard margarine, softened, for brushing top	1 tsp.	5 mL

Stir granulated sugar in first amount of warm water in small bowl. Sprinkle yeast over top. Let stand 10 minutes. Stir to dissolve yeast.

Measure next 5 ingredients into large bowl. Add yeast mixture. Stir well.

Add second amount of warm water and cooking oil. Stir. Dough will be sticky and soft. Spoon evenly into greased 9 × 5 × 3 inch (22 × 12 × 7 cm) loaf pan. Bake in 375°F (190°C) oven for about 45 minutes. Turn out onto rack to cool.

Brush warm top with butter. Makes 1 loaf.

1. Oatmeal Batter Bread, page 12
2. Rye Batter Bread, page 13
3. Nutri Batter Bread, page 11
4. Holiday Batter Bread, page 19
5. Brown Batter Bread, page 14

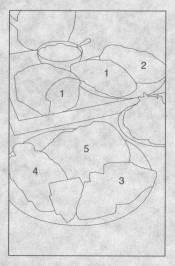

An easy-to-do loaf, full of fruit and very tasty.

Granulated sugar	1 tsp.	5 mL
Warm water	1/4 cup	60 mL
Active dry yeast	1 x 1/4 oz.	1 x 8 g
Milk	1/2 cup	125 mL
Butter or hard margarine	1/4 cup	60 mL
Granulated sugar	1/4 cup	60 mL
Salt	1 tsp.	5 mL
Cold water	1/4 cup	60 mL
Large egg, beaten	1	1
Raisins	3/4 cup	175 mL
Cut mixed glazed fruit	1 cup	250 mL
All-purpose flour	3 cups	750 mL

Stir first amount of sugar in warm water in small bowl. Sprinkle yeast over top. Let stand 10 minutes. Stir to dissolve yeast.

Scald milk in saucepan. Remove from heat.

Stir in butter, second amount of sugar and salt. Pour into large bowl.

Add cold water. Mix in egg, raisins and fruit. Add yeast mixture. Stir.

Add flour. Stir to moisten. Cover with greased waxed paper and tea towel. Let stand in oven with light on and door closed for 15 minutes. Spoon into greased 9 x 5 x 3 inch (22 x 12 x 7 cm) loaf pan. Cover with greased waxed paper and tea towel. Let stand in oven with light on and door closed about 1 1/4 hours until doubled in size. Bake in 350°F (175°C) oven for 30 to 35 minutes. Turn out onto rack to cool. Makes 1 loaf.

Pictured on page 17.

Every so often ghosts gather to swim in the Dead Sea.

MACHINE FRENCH BREAD

For a crispy crust, place a pan of water in the oven while baking.

Water	¾ cup	175 mL
Bread flour	2 cups	450 mL
Bread machine yeast	1½ tsp.	7 mL
Salt	1 tsp.	5 mL

Place all ingredients in bread machine in order given. Run machine through dough cycle. Remove dough. Roll into 10 inch (25 cm) log. Place on greased baking sheet that has been sprinkled with cornmeal. Using a sharp knife, make 3 diagonal cuts in tops. Cover with tea towel. Let stand in oven with light on and door closed for 45 minutes to 1 hour until doubled in size. Brush tops and sides with a mixture of 1 egg white, beaten, with a fork with 1 tbsp. (15 mL) water. Bake in 400°F (205°C) oven for about 15 to 18 minutes. Turn out onto rack to cool. Makes 1 loaf.

MACHINE CHALLAH

Let the bread machine do the kneading for you.

Water	⅔ cup	150 mL
Large egg	1	1
Cooking oil	2 tbsp.	30 mL
Bread flour	2 cups	450 mL
Dry milk powder	2 tbsp.	30 mL
Granulated sugar	1 tbsp.	15 mL
Bread machine yeast	1½ tsp.	7 mL
Salt	1 tsp.	5 mL
Large egg, fork-beaten	1	1
Water	1 tbsp.	15 mL

Place all ingredients in bread machine in order given. To make the traditional braid, remove dough after first kneading cycle. Divide in 3 parts. Roll each part into 16 inch (40 cm) long ropes. Place on greased baking sheet. Pinch 3 ends together. Braid the strips. Pinch ends together and tuck under. Cover with tea towel. Let stand in oven with light on and door closed for about 45 minutes until doubled in size.

Mix beaten egg and water. Brush over top of braid. Bake in 375°F (190°C) oven for about 25 minutes. Remove to rack to cool. Makes 1 loaf.

MACHINE BRAN BREAD

Light brown in color. Good breakfast bread.

MEDIUM LOAF		Ingredient	LARGE LOAF	
1/3 cup	75 mL	Natural bran (not cereal)	1/2 cup	125 mL
2/3 cup	150 mL	Water	1 cup	250 mL
1	1	Large egg, beaten	1	1
1 tbsp.	15 mL	Butter or hard margarine	1 1/2 tbsp.	25 mL
2 tbsp.	30 mL	Mild molasses	3 tbsp.	50 mL
1/2 cup	125 mL	Bread flour	3/4 cup	175 mL
1 1/4 cups	275 mL	Whole wheat flour	1 7/8 cups	470 mL
1 1/2 tsp.	7 mL	Bread machine yeast	2 1/4 tsp.	11 mL
1 tsp.	5 mL	Salt	1 1/2 tsp.	7 mL
3 tbsp.	45 mL	Raw, unsalted Sunflower seeds (optional)	4 1/2 tbsp.	68 mL

Place all ingredients in bread machine in order given. Follow manufacturer's instructions. Makes 1 loaf.

MACHINE REGULAR WHITE BREAD

Excellent taste and texture. Just right for sandwiches.

MEDIUM LOAF		Ingredient	LARGE LOAF	
3/4 cup	175 mL	Water or milk	1 1/8 cups	280 mL
1 tbsp.	15 mL	Butter or hard margarine	1 1/2 tbsp.	25 mL
1 3/4 cups	425 mL	Bread flour	2 2/3 cups	650 mL
1 tbsp.	15 mL	Granulated sugar	1 1/2 tbsp.	25 mL
3/4 tsp.	4 mL	Salt	1 tsp.	5 mL
1 1/2 tsp.	7 mL	Bread machine yeast	2 1/4 tsp.	11 mL

Place all ingredients in bread machine in order given. Follow manufacturer's instructions. Makes 1 loaf.

MACHINE ANADAMA BREAD

Medium loaf (1 lb or 450 g). Very light bread.

MEDIUM LOAF		Ingredient	LARGE LOAF	
2/3 cup	150 mL	Water	7/8 cup	200 mL
2 tbsp.	30 mL	Cornmeal	3 tbsp.	45 mL
1 1/2 tsp.	7 mL	Butter or hard margarine	2 tsp.	10 mL
2 tbsp.	30 mL	Mild molasses	2 1/2 tbsp.	37 mL
1 1/2 cups	175 mL	Bread flour	2 cups	450 mL
1/2 tsp.	2 mL	Salt	3/4 tsp.	4 mL
1 tsp.	5 mL	Bread machine yeast	1 1/2 tsp.	7 mL

Place all ingredients in bread machine in order given. Follow manufacturer's instructions. Makes 1 loaf.

MACHINE BLACK BREAD

Dark bread with a rich flavor.

MEDIUM LOAF			LARGE LOAF	
1 cup	225 mL	Water	1⅛ cups	280 mL
1 tbsp.	15 mL	Dark molasses	1½ tbsp.	25 mL
2 tsp.	10 mL	Cider vinegar	1 tbsp.	15 mL
2 tbsp.	30 mL	Butter or hard margarine	3 tbsp.	50 mL
1½ cups	350 mL	Bread flour	2¼ cups	560 mL
1 cup	225 mL	Rye flour	1½ cups	375 mL
1 tsp.	5 mL	Instant coffee granules	1½ tsp.	7 mL
2 tbsp.	30 mL	Cocoa	3 tbsp.	50 mL
½ tsp.	2 mL	Salt	¾ tsp.	4 mL
½ tsp.	2 mL	Caraway seeds (optional)	¾ tsp.	4 mL
¼ tsp.	1 mL	Fennel seeds	⅜ tsp.	2 mL
¼ tsp.	1 mL	Onion powder	⅜ tsp.	2 mL
1½ tsp.	7 mL	Bread machine yeast	2¼ tsp.	11 mL

Place all ingredients in bread machine in order given. Follow manufacturer's instructions. Makes 1 loaf.

MACHINE MULTI-GRAIN LOAF

Nutty, whole grain taste. Medium brown color with flecks of seeds showing.

MEDIUM LOAF			LARGE LOAF	
1 cup	225 mL	Water	1½ cups	375 mL
1 tbsp.	15 mL	Cooking oil	1½ tbsp.	25 mL
2 tbsp.	30 mL	Brown sugar, packed	3 tbsp.	50 mL
1 cup	225 mL	Bread flour	1½ cups	375 mL
¾ cup	175 mL	Whole wheat flour	1⅛ cups	280 mL
½ cup	125 mL	7 or 12 grain cereal (health food store)	¾ cup	175 mL
¼ cup	60 mL	Rolled oats (not instant)	6 tbsp.	100 mL
2 tsp.	10 mL	Bread machine yeast	1 tbsp.	15 mL
1 tsp.	5 mL	Salt	1½ tsp.	7 mL

Place all ingredients in bread machine in order given. Follow manufacturer's instructions. Makes 1 loaf.

MACHINE OATMEAL BREAD

Golden with flecks of oatmeal.

MEDIUM LOAF			LARGE LOAF	
¾ cup	175 mL	Water	1⅛ cups	280 mL
1 tbsp.	15 mL	Mild molasses	1½ tbsp.	25 mL
1 tbsp.	15 mL	Butter or hard margarine	5 tbsp.	80 mL
2 cups	450 mL	Bread flour	2⅔ cups	650 mL
⅓ cup	75 mL	Rolled oats	1⅓ cups	325 mL
1 tbsp.	15 mL	Brown sugar, packed	3 tbsp.	50 mL
1½ tsp.	7 mL	Bread machine yeast	2¼ tsp.	11 mL
¾ tsp.	4 mL	Salt	1¼ tsp.	6 mL

Place all ingredients in bread machine in order given. Follow manufacturer's instructions. Makes 1 loaf.

MACHINE CRACKED WHEAT BREAD

Crunchy bits of cracked wheat throughout, but nice and moist.

MEDIUM LOAF			LARGE LOAF	
1 cup	225 mL	Boiling water	1½ cups	375 mL
½ cup	125 mL	Cracked wheat	¾ cup	175 mL
1 tbsp.	15 mL	Butter or hard margarine	1½ tbsp.	25 mL
2 tbsp.	30 mL	Brown sugar, packed	3 tbsp.	50 mL
1¼ cup	300 mL	Bread flour	1¾ cups	425 mL
¾ cup	175 mL	Whole wheat flour	1½ cups	375 mL
2 tsp.	10 mL	Bread machine yeast	1 tbsp.	15 mL
½ tsp.	2 mL	Salt	¾ tsp.	4 mL

Combine boiling water and cracked wheat in small bowl. Let stand for 5 minutes. Water should be mostly absorbed. Put softened cracked wheat in bottom of bread machine.

Add remaining ingredients in order given. Follow manufacturer's instructions. Makes 1 loaf.

MACHINE SOURDOUGH BREAD

Wonderfully golden loaf with just a touch of "sour" to the taste.

MEDIUM LOAF			LARGE LOAF	
³⁄₄ cup	175 mL	Sourdough starter, see page 102	1¹⁄₈ cups	280 mL
³⁄₈ cup	90 mL	Milk	9 tbsp.	130 mL
1 tbsp.	15 mL	Butter or hard margarine	1¹⁄₂ tbsp.	25 mL
2 cups	450 mL	Bread flour	3 cups	750 mL
1¹⁄₂ tbsp.	25 mL	Granulated sugar	2¹⁄₄ tbsp.	38 mL
1¹⁄₂ tsp.	7 mL	Bread machine yeast	2¹⁄₄ tsp.	11 mL
1 tsp.	5 mL	Salt	1¹⁄₂ tsp.	7 mL

Place all ingredients in bread machine in order given. Follow manufacturer's instructions. Makes 1 loaf.

Pictured on page 35.

MACHINE 100% WHOLE WHEAT BREAD

Wonderfully wholesome!

MEDIUM LOAF			LARGE LOAF	
⁷⁄₈ cup	220 mL	Water	1 cup	225 mL
1¹⁄₂ tbsp.	25 mL	Mild molasses	2 tbsp.	30 mL
1 tbsp.	15 mL	Butter or hard margarine	1¹⁄₂ tbsp.	25 mL
2 cups	500 mL	Whole wheat flour	2¹⁄₂ cups	575 mL
1¹⁄₄ tsp.	7 mL	Bread machine yeast	1¹⁄₂ tsp.	7 mL
³⁄₄ tsp.	4 mL	Salt	1 tsp.	5 mL

Place all ingredients in bread machine in order given. Follow manufacturer's instructions. Makes 1 loaf.

Pictured on cover.

MACHINE SWEDISH RYE BREAD

Tang of orange peel is in both aroma and flavor.

MEDIUM LOAF			LARGE LOAF	
1 cup	225 mL	Water	1¹⁄₈ cup	280 mL
1 tbsp.	15 mL	Butter or hard margarine	3 tbsp.	50 mL
1³⁄₄ cups	400 mL	Bread flour	2³⁄₈ cups	600 mL
1 cup	225 mL	Rye flour	1¹⁄₂ cups	375 mL
3 tbsp.	45 mL	Brown sugar	¹⁄₄ cup	60 mL
1 tsp.	5 mL	Grated orange peel	1¹⁄₂ tsp.	7 mL
¹⁄₄ tsp.	1 mL	Fennel seeds	³⁄₈ tsp.	2 mL
³⁄₄ tsp.	4 mL	Salt	³⁄₄ tsp.	4 mL
1¹⁄₂ tsp.	7 mL	Bread machine yeast	2¹⁄₃ tsp.	11 mL

Place all ingredients in bread machine in order given. Follow manufacturer's instructions. Makes 1 loaf.

MACHINE PEPPERONI BREAD

Do not use delay cycle on this bread.

MEDIUM LOAF			LARGE LOAF	
7/8 cup	200 mL	Water	1 1/3 cups	325 mL
1 1/4 cups	300 mL	Bread flour	2 cups	500 mL
3/4 cup	175 mL	Whole wheat flour	1 cup	250 mL
1 tsp.	5 mL	Granulated sugar	1 1/2 tsp.	7 mL
1/4 tsp.	1 mL	Salt	1/2 tsp.	2 mL
1/8 tsp.	0.5 mL	Pepper	1/8 tsp.	0.5 mL
1/2 tsp.	2 mL	Parsley flakes	3/4 tsp.	4 mL
1 1/2 tsp.	7 mL	Bread machine yeast	2 1/4 tsp.	11 mL
1/3 cup	75 mL	Finely diced pepperoni	1/2 cup	125 mL

Place first 8 ingredients in bread machine in order given. Follow manufacturer's instructions.

Add pepperoni at raisin/nut signal or about 5 minutes before last kneading is finished. Makes 1 loaf.

Pictured on page 35.

MACHINE RYE BREAD

Light in color. Serve at lunch time with soup or at supper with a hearty casserole.

MEDIUM LOAF			LARGE LOAF	
7/8 cup	200 mL	Water	1 1/3 cups	325 mL
2 tbsp.	30 mL	Mild molasses	3 tbsp.	50 mL
2 tbsp.	30 mL	Butter or hard margarine	3 tbsp.	50 mL
1 1/2 cups	350 mL	Bread flour	2 1/4 cups	560 mL
1 cup	225 mL	Rye flour	1 1/2 cups	375 mL
1 1/2 tbsp.	25 mL	Granulated sugar	2 1/4 tbsp.	40 mL
1 1/2 tsp.	7 mL	Bread machine yeast	2 1/4 tsp.	11 mL
1/2 tsp.	2 mL	Salt	3/4 tsp.	4 mL
1 tsp.	5 mL	Caraway seeds (optional)	1 1/2 tsp.	7 mL

Place all ingredients in bread machine in order given. Follow manufacturer's instructions. Makes 1 loaf.

MACHINE PUMPERNICKEL

Excellent flavor. Serve with cream cheese or smoked meats.

MEDIUM LOAF			LARGE LOAF	
1 cup	225 mL	Water	1¼ cups	310 mL
2 tbsp.	30 mL	Butter or hard margarine	2½ tbsp.	40 mL
2 tbsp.	30 mL	Mild molasses	2½ tbsp.	40 mL
1½ cups	375 mL	Bread flour	2 cups	500 mL
1½ cup	375 mL	Rye flour	2 cups	500 mL
2 tbsp.	30 mL	Cocoa	2½ tbsp.	40 mL
1 tbsp.	15 mL	Brown sugar, packed	1½ tbsp.	25 mL
1 tsp.	5 mL	Caraway seeds (optional)	1¼ tsp.	6 mL
2 tsp.	10 mL	Bread machine yeast	2½ tsp.	12 mL
¾ tsp.	4 mL	Salt	1 tsp.	5 mL
½ tsp.	2 mL	Instant coffee granules	¾ tsp.	4 mL

Place all ingredients in bread machine in order given. Follow manufacturer's instructions. Makes 1 loaf.

Pictured on page 35.

MACHINE FRUIT BREAD

Serve with slices of cheddar cheese.

MEDIUM LOAF			LARGE LOAF	
½ cup	125 mL	Milk	⅞ cup	220 mL
1		1 Large egg, beaten	1	1
3 tbsp.	45 mL	Butter or hard margarine	4½ tbsp.	70 mL
2 cups	450 mL	Bread flour	3 cups	750 mL
3 tbsp.	45 mL	Granulated sugar	4½ tbsp.	70 mL
½ tsp.	2 mL	Salt	¾ tsp.	4 mL
1½ tsp.	7 mL	Bread machine yeast	2¼ tsp.	11 mL
2 tbsp.	30 mL	Light raisins	3 tbsp.	50 mL
2 tbsp.	30 mL	Dark raisins	3 tbsp.	50 mL
⅓ cup	75 mL	Cut mixed glazed fruit	½ cup	125 mL

Place first 7 ingredients in bread machine in order given.

Add next 3 fruits after the beep that follows the raisin bread cycle. Follow manufacturer's instructions. Makes 1 loaf.

Pictured on page 35.

MACHINE COTTAGE DILL BREAD

Nice golden appearance with flecks of onion and dill showing.

MEDIUM LOAF			LARGE LOAF	
²/₃ cup	150 mL	Creamed cottage cheese	1 cup	250 mL
3 tbsp.	45 mL	Water	4¹/₂ tbsp.	70 mL
1 tbsp.	15 mL	Butter or hard margarine	1¹/₂ tbsp.	25 mL
1	1	Large egg	1	1
2 cups	450 mL	Bread flour	3 cups	750 mL
1 tbsp.	15 mL	Granulated sugar	1¹/₂ tbsp.	25 mL
1 tbsp.	15 mL	Onion flakes	1¹/₂ tbsp.	25 mL
1¹/₂ tsp.	7 mL	Bread machine yeast	2¹/₄ tsp.	11 mL
2 tsp.	10 mL	Dill weed	1 tbsp.	15 mL
³/₄ tsp.	4 mL	Salt	1 tsp.	5 mL

Place all ingredients in bread machine in order given. Follow manufacturer's instructions. Makes 1 loaf.

Pictured on cover.

MACHINE HERB BREAD

Excellent with soups or in making sandwiches.

MEDIUM LOAF			LARGE LOAF	
⁷/₈ cup	200 mL	Water	1¹/₄ cups	300 mL
1 tbsp.	15 mL	Butter or hard margarine	1¹/₂ tbsp.	25 mL
2 cups	450 mL	Bread flour	3¹/₄ cups	810 mL
1 tbsp.	15 mL	Granulated sugar	1¹/₂ tbsp.	25 mL
1 tbsp.	15 mL	Dry milk powder	1¹/₂ tbsp.	25 mL
¹/₄ tsp.	1 mL	Ground thyme	³/₈ tsp.	2 mL
¹/₄ tsp.	1 mL	Garlic powder	³/₈ tsp.	2 mL
¹/₂ tsp.	2 mL	Whole oregano	³/₄ tsp.	4 mL
¹/₄ tsp.	1 mL	Onion powder	³/₈ tsp.	2 mL
1¹/₂ tsp.	7 mL	Bread machine yeast	2¹/₄ tsp.	11 mL
¹/₂ tsp.	2 mL	Salt	³/₄ tsp.	4 mL

Place all ingredients in bread machine in order given. Follow manufacturer's instructions. Makes 1 loaf.

Pictured on page 35.

COFFEE CAKE SWIRL

Great for the beginner. Fancy but simple.

Milk	1 cup	250 mL
Butter or hard margarine	¼ cup	60 mL
Grated orange rind	1 tbsp.	15 mL
Granulated sugar	⅓ cup	75 mL
Salt	¾ tsp.	4 mL
All-purpose flour	1½ cups	375 mL
Instant yeast	1 x ¼ oz.	1 x 8 g
Large egg, beaten	1	1
All-purpose flour	1½ cups	375 mL
RAISIN FILLING		
Raisins	1 cup	250 mL
Water	½ cup	125 mL
Lemon juice, fresh or bottled	2 tsp.	10 mL
Brown sugar, packed	½ cup	125 mL
All-purpose flour	⅓ cup	75 mL
Salt	⅛ tsp.	0.5 mL
Milk	2 tsp.	10 mL
GLAZE		
Icing (confectioner's) sugar	¾ cup	175 mL
Frozen concentrated orange juice, thawed	4 tsp.	20 mL

Scald milk in saucepan. Remove from heat.

Stir in butter, orange rind, sugar and salt until butter melts and sugar dissolves. Pour into large bowl.

Add first amount of flour, yeast and egg. Beat until mixed.

Work in remaining flour. Turn out onto floured surface. Knead 5 to 7 minutes. Cover with tea towel. Let stand on counter while preparing filling.

Raisin Filling: Place raisins, water and lemon juice in saucepan. Boil slowly for 1 minute.

Mix brown sugar, flour and salt together well in small bowl. Stir into raisin mixture. Stir and boil until thickened. Cool by placing saucepan in cold water. Stir often.

(continued on next page)

Roll dough into 24 x 4 inch (60 x 10 cm) rectangle. Spoon filling down center. Join edges of dough by pinching. Have both ends tapered. Beginning in center on greased baking sheet make a coiled spiral, seam side down. Pinch outside end to loaf. Cover with tea towel. Let stand in oven with light on and door closed for about 40 minutes until doubled in size.

Brush with milk. Bake in 350°F (175°C) oven for 20 to 25 minutes. Place on rack to cool.

Glaze: Stir icing sugar and orange juice in small bowl adding more icing sugar or orange juice to make a barely pourable glaze. Drizzle over cooled spiral loaf. Makes 1 loaf.

SALLY LUNN

A large golden ring of bread.

Granulated sugar	**1 tsp.**	**5 mL**
Warm water	**½ cup**	**125 mL**
Active dry yeast	**1 x ¼ oz.**	**1 x 8 g**
Butter or hard margarine, softened	**½ cup**	**125 mL**
Large eggs	**3**	**3**
Granulated sugar	**½ cup**	**125 mL**
All-purpose flour	**4 cups**	**1 L**
Salt	**1 tsp.**	**5 mL**
Milk	**1 cup**	**250 mL**

Stir first amount of sugar in water in small bowl. Sprinkle yeast over top. Let stand 10 minutes. Stir to dissolve yeast.

Beat butter, eggs, and second amount of sugar in large bowl.

Add flour, salt, milk and yeast mixture. Beat on low to moisten. Beat on medium for 2 minutes. Cover with greased waxed paper and tea towel. Let stand in oven with light on and door closed for about 1 hour until doubled in bulk. Stir dough down. Spoon into greased 10 inch (25 cm) angel food tube pan. Cover with greased waxed paper and tea towel. Let stand in oven with light on and door closed for about 30 minutes until almost doubled in size. Bake in 350°F (175°C) oven for 40 to 50 minutes until golden brown. Turn out onto serving plate. Slice with serrated knife. Serve hot. Makes 1 loaf.

FRUIT LOAF

A sprinkling of raisins and fruit give this a good flavor and a cheery look.

SPONGE

Milk	1½ cups	375 mL
Granulated sugar	1 tsp.	5 mL
Warm water	¼ cup	60 mL
Active dry yeast	1 × ¼ oz.	1 × 8 g
All-purpose flour	2 cups	500 mL
Granulated sugar	¼ cup	60 mL
Salt	1 tsp.	5 mL
Baking soda	¼ tsp.	1 mL

DOUGH

Butter or hard margarine, softened	¼ cup	60 mL
Granulated sugar	¼ cup	60 mL
Large egg	1	1
Raisins	1 cup	250 mL
Cut mixed glazed fruit	½ cup	125 mL
Ground cinnamon	¼ tsp.	1 mL
Ground mace	⅛ tsp.	0.5 mL
All-purpose flour, approximately	3½ cups	875 mL

Sponge: Scald milk in saucepan. Cool to lukewarm.

Stir first amount of sugar in warm water in small bowl. Sprinkle yeast over top. Let stand 10 minutes. Stir to dissolve yeast.

Measure first amount of flour, second amount of sugar, salt and baking soda into large bowl. Stir. Add milk and yeast mixture. Beat on low to moisten. Beat on medium for 4 to 5 minutes until springy. Cover with greased waxed paper and tea towel. Let stand in oven with light on and door closed for 1¼ hours.

Dough: Cream butter and third amount of sugar in separate bowl. Beat in egg. Add to sponge.

Add raisins, fruit, cinnamon and mace. Mix.

(continued on next page)

Work in enough remaining flour until dough pulls away from sides of bowl. Turn out onto floured surface. Knead 8 to 10 minutes until smooth and elastic. Place in greased bowl, turning once to grease top. Cover with tea towel. Let stand in oven with light on and door closed about 1¼ hours until doubled in bulk. Punch dough down. Divide and shape into 2 loaves. Place in 2 greased 9 x 5 x 3 inch (22 x 12 x 7 cm) loaf pans. Cover with tea towel. Let stand in oven with light on and door closed about 45 minutes until doubled in size. Bake in 350°F (175°C) oven for about 40 minutes. Turn out onto racks to cool. Makes 2 loaves.

BUTTERSCOTCH PULL-APARTS

Sticky and delicious.

Loaf of frozen bread dough	1	1
Chopped walnuts	¼ cup	60 mL
Raisins	¼ cup	60 mL
Brown sugar, packed	⅓ cup	75 mL
Butterscotch pudding powder, (not instant) about ½ package	⅓ cup	75 mL
Butter or hard margarine, melted	6 tbsp.	100 mL
Ground cinnamon, sprinkle		

Thaw bread loaf for 1½ hours. Cut into ½ inch (12 mm) slices.

Sprinkle walnuts and raisins in bottom of greased 12 cup (2.7 L) bundt pan. Overlap pieces of dough in a ring.

Sprinkle brown sugar and pudding powder over dough. Pour melted butter over top.

Sprinkle with cinnamon. Cover tightly with plastic wrap. Let rise overnight on kitchen counter for 10 to 12 hours or until doubled in size. Bake in 350°F (175°C) oven for about 30 minutes. Let cool on rack for 5 minutes. Turn out onto serving plate. Serves 6 to 8 people.

PANETTONE

This fruity pah-neh-TOH-nee is flavored with anise. Ideal with tea or coffee or for an evening snack.

Large eggs	3	3
Warm milk	½ cup	125 mL
Butter or hard margarine, softened	6 tbsp.	100 mL
Boiling water	⅔ cup	150 mL
Vanilla	1 tsp.	5 mL
All-purpose flour	2 cups	500 mL
Granulated sugar	½ cup	125 mL
Instant yeast	2 × ¼ oz.	2 × 8 g
Salt	1½ tsp.	7 mL
Anise seeds (or 1 tsp., 5 mL, anise flavoring)	1 tsp.	5 mL
All-purpose flour, approximately	3½ cups	875 mL
Light-colored raisins	¾ cup	175 mL
Medium-colored raisins	¾ cup	175 mL
Pine nuts	½ cup	125 mL
Cut mixed glazed fruit	½ cup	125 mL
Grated lemon peel	1 tsp.	5 mL
Butter or hard margarine, softened	1 tbsp.	15 mL

Beat eggs in large bowl.

Add milk. Stir in butter. Add boiling water and vanilla. Mix.

Add next 5 ingredients. Beat on low to moisten. Beat on medium until smooth.

Work in as much flour as needed until dough pulls away from sides of bowl.

Stir in both types of raisins, pine nuts, fruit and peel. Knead dough 6 to 8 minutes. Place in greased bowl, turning once to grease top. Cover with tea towel. Let stand in oven with light on and door closed for about 1½ hours until doubled in bulk. Punch dough down. Divide into 2 equal portions. Shape into round loaves. Place on greased baking sheet. Cover with tea towel. Let stand in oven with light on and door closed for about 1 hour until doubled in size. Bake in 350°F (175°C) oven for about 35 minutes. Place on racks to cool.

Brush warm tops with butter. Makes 2 loaves.

Pictured on page 53.

So easy and so good. A light texture.

Granulated sugar	1 tsp.	5 mL
Warm water	1/4 cup	60 mL
Active dry yeast	1 x 1/4 oz.	1 x 8 g
Milk	1 1/2 cups	375 mL
Granulated sugar	1/3 cup	75 mL
Salt	1 1/2 tsp.	7 mL
Large egg	1	1
All-purpose flour	1 cup	250 mL
Butter or hard margarine, melted	1/4 cup	60 mL
Cold butter (not margarine)	1 cup	250 mL
All-purpose flour	4 cups	1 L
Large egg	1	1
Water	1 tbsp.	15 mL

Stir first amount of sugar and warm water together in small bowl. Sprinkle yeast over top. Let stand 10 minutes. Stir to dissolve yeast.

Measure next 6 ingredients into medium bowl. Add yeast mixture. Beat until smooth.

Cut second amount of butter into second amount of flour in large bowl until it is the size of large shelled peanuts. Add yeast mixture. Use a rubber spatula to fold together just until flour is moistened. Divide dough into 4 equal portions. Place all 4 portions in bowl. Cover with tea towel. Chill in refrigerator for 15 minutes. Remove 1 portion at a time from refrigerator. Roll on lightly floured board into 16 to 17 inch (41 to 43 cm) circle. Cut into 8 wedges. Starting at wide end, roll loosely towards point. Arrange, point side down, on ungreased baking sheet, shaping into crescent. Leave 2 inch (5 cm) space between each roll. Cover with tea towel. Let stand in oven with light on and door closed for 1 1/2 to 2 hours until almost doubled in size.

Beat egg with remaining water in small bowl with fork. Brush over each roll. Bake in 375°F (190°C) oven for about 15 minutes. Remove to racks to cool. Makes 32.

Pictured on page 53.

WHOLE WHEAT PITA

These are fun to make. Cut in half and fill "pockets" with a sandwich filling, or cut into pieces and serve as a "cracker".

Whole wheat flour	**2 cups**	**500 mL**
Active dry yeast	**1 x ¼ oz.**	**1 x 8 g**
Warm water	**1¼ cups**	**300 mL**
Salt	**½ tsp.**	**2 mL**
All-purpose flour, approximately	**1½ cups**	**375 mL**

Measure first 4 ingredients into large bowl. Mix well.

Work in enough remaining flour until dough pulls away from sides of bowl. Turn out onto floured surface. Knead 4 to 5 minutes until smooth and elastic. Cut and shape into 10 balls. Roll out each ball ¼ inch (6 mm) thick and 5 to 6 inches (12 to 15 cm) in diameter on lightly floured surface. Both sides should be lightly covered with flour. Place on ungreased non-stick baking sheet or a cornmeal dusted regular sheet. Cover with tea towel. Let stand in oven with light on and door closed about 35 minutes. Bake in 500°F (260°C) oven on bottom rack for 5 minutes. Repeat until all are baked. Wrap in tea towel for 3 minutes as they are removed from oven. Cool. Makes 10.

Pictured on page 89.

1. Machine Herb Bread, page 27
2. Machine Pumpernickel, page 26
3. Machine Sourdough Bread, page 24
4. Machine Pepperoni Bread, page 25
5. Machine Fruit Bread, page 26

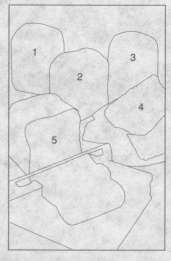

Flowers Courtesy Of:
Eaton's Housewares Dept.

Linen Courtesy Of:
Enchanted Kitchen and La Cache

Bread Boards Courtesy Of:
Le Gnome

This KOO-kehn is absolutely delicious. Layers of apples in a good crust.

Granulated sugar	1 tsp.	5 mL
Warm water	1/4 cup	60 mL
Active dry yeast	1 x 1/4 oz.	1 x 8 g
Milk	1 cup	250 mL
Butter or hard margarine, melted	1/2 cup	125 mL
Granulated sugar	1/2 cup	125 mL
Salt	1/2 tsp.	2 mL
All-purpose flour	2 cups	500 mL
Large egg, beaten	1	1
All-purpose flour	2 cups	500 mL
TOPPING		
Cooking apples, cored, peeled and sliced (McIntosh is good)	4	4
Butter or hard margarine	1/4 cup	60 mL
Granulated sugar	1 cup	250 mL
Ground cinnamon	1 tsp.	5 mL

Stir first amount of sugar in warm water in large bowl. Sprinkle yeast over top. Let stand 10 minutes. Stir to dissolve yeast.

Add next 4 ingredients.

Add first amount of flour and egg. Beat until smooth.

Add second amount of flour. Beat until smooth. Cover. Chill in refrigerator for 2 hours. Divide dough into 2 equal portions. Press each portion into greased 9 x 9 inch (22 x 22 cm) pans, pressing up sides to make edges.

Topping: Lay apple slices in rows over top of dough.

Melt butter in saucepan. Stir in third amount of sugar and cinnamon. Sprinkle 1/2 over apples in each pan. Bake in 375°F (190°C) oven for about 35 minutes. Serve warm or cold. Each pan cuts into 9 generous pieces.

Pictured on page 53.

EASTER EGG BREAD

Pretty as a picture. Easier than it looks.

Granulated sugar	2 tsp.	10 mL
Warm water	1/2 cup	125 mL
Active dry yeast	2 x 1/4 oz.	2 x 8 g
All-purpose flour	1 cup	250 mL
Warm water	1/3 cup	75 mL
Butter or hard margarine, softened	3/4 cup	175 mL
Grated lemon peel	1 tbsp.	15 mL
Lemon juice, fresh or bottled	1 1/2 tbsp.	25 mL
Granulated sugar	3/4 cup	175 mL
Salt	1/2 tsp.	2 mL
Eggs, beaten	2	2
All-purpose flour, approximately	4 cups	1 L
Eggs, raw and colored (see Note)	6	6
ICING		
Butter or hard margarine, softened	2 tbsp.	30 mL
Icing (confectioner's) sugar	1 cup	250 mL
Water	1 1/2 tbsp.	25 mL
Vanilla	1/2 tsp.	2 mL

Stir first amount of sugar in warm water in small bowl. Sprinkle yeast over top. Let stand 10 minutes. Stir to dissolve yeast. Pour into large bowl.

Add first amount of flour and mix. Add warm water. Beat until smooth. Cover with tea towel. Let stand in oven with light on and door closed about 30 minutes until doubled in bulk.

Beat butter, lemon peel, lemon juice, sugar and salt together in large bowl until fluffy. Add beaten eggs and beat well.

Add yeast mixture and beat. Mix in about half of the second amount of flour. Work in enough remaining flour until dough pulls away from sides of bowl. Turn out onto floured surface. Knead 8 to 10 minutes until smooth and elastic. Place in greased bowl, turning once to grease top. Cover with tea towel. Let stand in oven with light on and door closed about 1 1/2 hours until doubled in bulk. Punch dough down. Divide into 3 equal balls. Shape each ball into a rope about 2 feet (60 cm) long. Form the 3 ropes into a loose braid, then shape into a circle on greased baking sheet. Pinch ends together.

(continued on next page)

Tuck eggs into 6 pockets made by spreading braids apart enough to make room. Cover with tea towel. Let stand in oven with light on and door closed about 45 minutes until doubled in size. Bake in 375°F (190°C) oven for about 30 minutes. Place on rack to cool.

Icing: Beat all ingredients together adding a bit more water or sugar if needed to make proper spreading consistency. Spread over egg bread. Makes 1 ring.

Note: To color uncooked eggs, mix ½ cup (125 mL) boiling water, 1 tsp. (5 mL) vinegar and ¼ tsp. (1 mL) food coloring in small bowl. Dip eggs until desired color is reached. Remove and allow to dry. Brush dried shells with cooking oil before inserting into braid.

Pictured on page 53.

STREUSEL COFFEE CAKE

Lightly-spiced flavor with a crunchy top.

All-purpose flour	2½ cups	625 mL
Granulated sugar	¾ cup	175 mL
Brown sugar, packed	1 cup	250 mL
Ground nutmeg	1 tsp.	5 mL
Salt	½ tsp.	2 mL
Cooking oil	¾ cup	175 mL
Buttermilk, fresh or reconstituted from powder	1¼ cups	300 mL
Large egg, beaten	1	1
Baking soda	1 tsp.	5 mL
Water	1 tsp.	5 mL
Chopped walnuts or pecans	½ cup	125 mL
Ground cinnamon	2 tsp.	10 mL
Reserved dry ingredients	½ cup	125 mL

Mix first 6 ingredients in large bowl. Measure ½ cup (125 mL) of mixture and set aside in small bowl.

Add buttermilk and egg to flour mixture in large bowl. Stir.

Dissolve baking soda in water in small cup. Add to mixture in large bowl. Stir. Spread in 9 x 9 inch (22 x 22 cm) greased pan.

Add walnuts and cinnamon to reserved dry ingredients in small bowl. Sprinkle over top. Bake in 325°F (160°C) oven for 45 to 50 minutes until an inserted wooden pick comes out clean. Makes 1 coffee cake.

Pictured on page 53.

TWO-TONE LOAF

This is a conversation piece. A white loaf is encircled with a dark cover.

WHITE DOUGH

All-purpose flour	1½ cups	375 mL
Granulated sugar	3 tbsp.	50 mL
Instant yeast	1 x ¼ oz.	1 x 8 g
Salt	1 tsp.	5 mL
Water	¾ cup	175 mL
Milk	½ cup	125 mL
Butter or hard margarine	1½ tbsp.	25 mL
All-purpose flour, approximately	2 cups	500 mL

DARK DOUGH

All-purpose flour	1 cup	250 mL
Granulated sugar	¼ cup	60 mL
Cocoa	¼ cup	60 mL
Instant yeast	1 x ¼ oz.	1 x 8 g
Salt	1 tsp.	5 mL
Water	1⅛ cups	275 mL
Dark molasses	2 tbsp.	30 mL
Instant coffee granules	1 tsp.	5 mL
Butter	2 tbsp.	30 mL
Rye flour, approximately	2 cups	500 mL
Butter or hard margarine, softened, for brushing tops	2 tsp.	10 mL

White Dough: Combine first amount of flour, sugar, yeast and salt in large bowl.

Heat and stir water, milk and butter in saucepan until a drop on your inner wrist feels quite warm. Pour slowly into flour mixture beating on medium-low as you pour. Beat on medium-high for 2 minutes.

Work in enough remaining flour until dough pulls away from sides of bowl. Knead 8 to 10 minutes until smooth and elastic. Place in greased bowl, turning once to grease top. Cover with tea towel. Let stand in oven with light on and door closed for about 1¾ hours until doubled in bulk.

(continued on next page)

Dark Dough: Combine first 5 ingredients in large bowl.

Heat and stir water, molasses, coffee granules and butter in saucepan until a drop on your inner wrist feels quite warm. Pour slowly into flour mixture beating on medium-low as you pour. Beat on medium-high for 2 minutes.

Work in enough rye flour until dough pulls away from sides of bowl. Knead 8 to 10 minutes until smooth and elastic. Place in greased bowl, turning once to grease top. Cover with tea towel. Let stand in oven with light on and door closed for about 1¾ hours until doubled in bulk.

Punch down both doughs. Divide both doughs in half. Shape white dough into 2 loaves. Roll out dark dough large enough to fit around each white loaf. Pinch ends. Place in 2 greased 9 x 5 x 3 inch (22 x 12 x 7 cm) loaf pans seam side down. Cover with tea towel. Let stand in oven with light on and door closed for about 45 minutes until doubled in size. Bake in 375°F (190°C) oven for about 25 minutes. Turn out onto racks to cool. Dark shell may have the odd crack as it is not possible to predict how it will rise.

Brush warm tops with butter. Makes 2 loaves.

Pictured on page 53.

Wide open eyes are a real asset before marriage but keep them half closed afterwards.

BRIOCHE

*Whether you are into cute, different or flavorful, and whether you say
BREE-ohsh or bree-AHSH, this recipe will fill the bill.*

Granulated sugar	1 tsp.	5 mL
Warm water	1/4 cup	60 mL
Active dry yeast	1 x 1/4 oz.	1 x 8 g
Butter or hard margarine, softened	1/2 cup	125 mL
Granulated sugar	1/3 cup	75 mL
Large eggs	3	3
Egg yolk (large), egg white reserved	1	1
Salt	3/4 tsp.	4 mL
All-purpose flour	2 1/2 cups	625 mL
Milk, scalded and cooled to lukewarm	3/4 cup	175 mL
All-purpose flour, approximately	2 3/4 cups	675 mL
Reserved egg white (large)	1	1
Granulated sugar	1 tbsp.	15 mL

Stir first amount of sugar in warm water in small bowl. Sprinkle yeast
over top. Let stand 10 minutes. Stir to dissolve yeast.

Cream butter and second amount of sugar in large bowl. Beat in
eggs and extra egg yolk 1 at a time. Add salt, first amount of flour
and yeast mixture. Beat on high until smooth.

Add milk. Mix. Work in enough flour until dough pulls away from sides
of bowl. Turn out onto floured surface. Knead 8 to 10 minutes until
smooth and elastic. Place in greased bowl, turning once to grease
top. Cover with tea towel. Let stand in oven with light on and door
closed for about 2 hours until doubled in bulk. Punch dough down.
Divide dough into 3 equal portions. Cut and shape each portion
into 7 egg-size pieces. Pinch a marble-size piece off each (about
1/8 of whole piece). Shape into a tiny bun. Shape remaining larger
piece into bun and put into greased brioche bun cups or muffin
cups. Use handle of teaspoon (or finger) to poke a hole through to
bottom. Spread hole slightly. Insert tiny bun partway into hole.
Repeat. Cover with tea towel. Let stand in oven with light on and
door closed for about 1 hour until doubled in size.

Beat egg white and sugar together. Brush tops of buns including
top-knots. Bake in 375°F (190°C) oven for about 15 minutes. Makes
21 brioche buns.

Pictured on page 53.

(continued on next page)

BRIOCHE LOAF: Divide batter into 3 portions. Using ⅛ of each portion, make a ball to insert in center. Place each large portion in greased brioche pans. Poke a hole in centers and insert balls. When risen, bake about 20 minutes. If buns or loaves brown too fast, lay foil over top. Makes 3 loaves.

DANISH COFFEE CAKE

Just right for a brunch, lunch or coffee party.

Granulated sugar	2 tbsp.	30 mL
Warm water	½ cup	125 mL
Active dry yeast	1 x ¼ oz.	1 x 8 g
Large eggs, beaten	2	2
All-purpose flour	2½ cups	625 mL
Butter or hard margarine	1 cup	250 mL
Salt	½ tsp.	2 mL
FILLING		
Butter or hard margarine, softened	½ cup	125 mL
Icing (confectioner's) sugar	1 cup	250 mL
All-purpose flour	2 tsp.	10 mL
Almond flavoring	2 tsp.	10 mL
Milk, for brushing tops	2 tsp.	10 mL
Granulated sugar, sprinkle		

Stir sugar in warm water in small bowl. Sprinkle yeast over top. Let stand 10 minutes. Stir to dissolve yeast.

Add beaten eggs. Stir.

Mix flour, butter and salt in medium bowl until crumbly. Add yeast mixture. Stir. Divide in half. Roll out each portion into long narrow rectangle 8 x 16 inches (20 x 40 cm).

Filling: Beat first 4 ingredients together well in small bowl. Spread ½ filling down center of each portion. Cut side of dough into 1 inch (2.5 cm) strips about ¼ inch (6 mm) from filling. Overlap strips from top to bottom. Fold up ends. Place on greased baking sheet.

Brush tops with milk. Sprinkle with sugar. Cover with tea towel. Let stand in oven with light on and door closed for 1 hour. Bake in 350°F (175°C) for about 25 to 30 minutes. Makes 2 coffee cakes.

Pictured on cover.

PINEAPPLE BREAD

A large loaf with bits of pineapple. Moist and flavorful.

Canned crushed pineapple	14 oz.	398 mL
Pineapple juice, plus water, if necessary	1 cup	250 mL
Granulated sugar	¼ cup	60 mL
Active dry yeast	1 × ¼ oz.	1 × 8 g
Fine coconut	½ cup	125 mL
All-purpose flour	1½ cups	375 mL
Salt	1 tsp.	5 mL
Baking soda	¼ tsp.	1 mL
Large egg	1	1
Reserved pineapple		
All-purpose flour, approximately	2¾ cups	685 mL
Butter or hard margarine, softened, for brushing top	1 tsp.	5 mL

Drain pineapple juice into measuring cup. Press pineapple to remove all juice. Reserve pineapple.

Pour pineapple juice and water into saucepan. Stir in sugar. Heat until warm. Remove from heat. Sprinkle yeast over top. Let stand 10 minutes. Stir to dissolve yeast. Turn into large bowl.

Add next 5 ingredients. Beat until smooth.

Add pineapple. Mix in.

Work in enough remaining flour until dough pulls away from sides of bowl. Knead 8 to 10 minutes until smooth and elastic. Place in greased bowl, turning once to grease top. Cover with tea towel. Let stand in oven with light on and door closed for about 1½ hours until doubled in bulk. Punch dough down. Shape into loaf. Place in greased 9 x 5 x 3 inch (22 x 12 x 7 cm) loaf pan. Cover with tea towel. Let stand in oven with light on and door closed for about 30 minutes until doubled in size. Bake in 375°F (190°C) oven for about 25 minutes. Turn out onto rack to cool.

Brush warm top with butter. Makes 1 loaf.

So attractive. So sweet. So good. An easy variation.

Granulated sugar	1 tsp.	5 mL
Warm water	¼ cup	60 mL
Active dry yeast	1 x ¼ oz.	1 x 8 g
All-purpose flour	4 cups	1L
Granulated sugar	¼ cup	60 mL
Salt	1 tsp.	5 mL
Butter or hard margarine, cold	1¼ cups	300 mL
Large eggs	2	2
Milk, scalded and cooled to lukewarm	1 cup	250 mL
Large egg, beaten, for brushing tops	1	1
Lemon cheese, orange jam or red jam or jelly	16 tsp.	80 mL
Finely chopped walnuts or pecans	⅓ cup	75 mL

Stir first amount of sugar in warm water in small bowl. Sprinkle yeast over top. Let stand 10 minutes. Stir to dissolve yeast.

Place next 3 ingredients in large bowl. Cut in butter until size of small peas.

Beat first 2 eggs in small bowl. Add warm milk. Add yeast mixture. Stir. Add to flour mixture. Mix with fork until it forms a ball. Dough will be sticky. Place in greased bowl, turning once to grease top. Cover with greased waxed paper and tea towel. Refrigerate for about 6 hours or overnight. Divide dough in half. Roll out on floured surface ½ inch (12 mm) thick. Cut into 4 inch (10 cm) squares. Fold each corner almost to center. Press or pinch down to make a depression. Place on greased baking sheet 2 inches (5 cm) apart.

Brush with egg. Put 1 tsp. lemon cheese or jam in center. Sprinkle with walnuts if desired. Cover with greased waxed paper and tea towel. Let stand on counter for 15 minutes. Bake in 400°F (205°C) oven for about 20 minutes until golden brown. Makes 16 pastries.

Pictured on page 53.

Variation: Place a ½ inch (12 mm) cube of cream cheese in center of folds before filling with jam.

Variation: When pastries have cooled, dust with icing sugar or drizzle with Glaze, page 64.

BUTTERHORNS

Good flavor and very tender. A family tradition. Serve toasted with hot chocolate.

Milk	**2 cups**	**500 mL**
Granulated sugar	**½ cup**	**125 mL**
Butter or hard margarine	**1 cup**	**250 mL**
Salt	**1 tsp.**	**5 mL**
Granulated sugar	**1 tsp.**	**5 mL**
Warm water	**½ cup**	**125 mL**
Active dry yeast	**1 × ¼ oz.**	**1 × 8 g**
All-purpose flour	**6 cups**	**1.5 L**
Large egg, beaten	**1**	**1**
ICING		
Icing (confectioner's) sugar	**2 cups**	**500 mL**
Butter or hard margarine, softened	**3 tbsp.**	**50 mL**
Milk or water	**2 tbsp.**	**30 mL**
Vanilla	**1 tsp.**	**5 mL**
Shaved almonds or finely chopped walnuts	**½ cup**	**125 mL**

Scald milk in saucepan. Remove from heat.

Add next 3 ingredients. Stir to dissolve sugar and melt butter. Cool to lukewarm.

Stir second amount of sugar in warm water in small bowl. Sprinkle yeast over top. Let stand 10 minutes. Stir to dissolve yeast.

Measure flour into large bowl. Make a well. Pour beaten egg into well. Add yeast mixture and milk mixture. Mix with spoon to moisten. Beat with spoon until mixed well. Cover with greased waxed paper and tea towel. Let stand in oven with light on and door closed for about 1 hour until doubled in bulk. Gently stir down with a spoon. Cover with greased waxed paper and tea towel. Let stand in oven with light on and door closed for about 30 minutes until doubled in bulk. Stir dough down. Divide dough into 2 portions. Roll out one portion on floured surface to 10 x 12 inch (25 x 30 cm) rectangle. Cut into 12 strips. Take each strip and roll lightly to smooth sides. Beginning with one end being the center, coil rest of strip around it. Pinch end to side of coil. Place 2 inches (5 cm) apart on greased baking sheet. Repeat with other portions. Cover with greased waxed paper and tea towel. Let stand in oven with light on and door closed for about 30 minutes until doubled in size. Bake in 375°F (190°C) oven for about 20 minutes. Place on racks to cool.

(continued on next page)

Icing: Mix first 4 ingredients together well adding more icing sugar or milk for proper spreading consistency. Spread icing over center of butterhorns, covering about two thirds.

Sprinkle with almonds or walnuts. Makes 24.

Pictured on page 53.

CINNAMON COFFEE CAKE

Very attractive with nutty streusel topping. Serve at brunch, lunch or afternoon get-together.

FILLING		
Brown sugar, packed	½ cup	125 mL
Chopped walnuts or pecans	½ cup	125 mL
Ground cinnamon	1½ tsp.	7 mL
CAKE		
Butter or hard margarine, softened	¾ cup	175 mL
Granulated sugar	1½ cups	375 mL
Large eggs	3	3
Vanilla	1½ tsp.	7 mL
All-purpose flour	3 cups	750 mL
Baking powder	1½ tsp.	7 mL
Baking soda	1 tsp.	5 mL
Salt	¼ tsp.	1 mL
Sour cream	1½ cups	375 mL

Filling: Mix all 3 ingredients in small bowl. Set aside.

Cake: Cream butter and sugar in large bowl. Beat in eggs 1 at a time. Add vanilla. Mix.

Stir flour, baking powder, baking soda and salt in medium bowl.

Add flour mixture to egg mixture in 3 parts alternately with sour cream in 2 parts beginning and ending with flour. Sprinkle ⅓ reserved filling in greased 10 inch (25 cm) angel food pan. Spoon ½ cake batter over top. Sprinkle with ⅓ filling. Spoon on second ½ cake batter. Top with remaining ⅓ filling. Bake in 350°F (175°C) oven for 50 to 60 minutes. Makes 1 large coffee cake.

Pictured on cover.

CINNAMON PUFFS

Such a wonderful treat. These disappear quickly.

Milk	1 cup	250 mL
Quick-cooking rolled oats (not instant)	1 cup	250 mL
Butter or hard margarine	¼ cup	60 mL
Granulated sugar	¼ cup	60 mL
Salt	1½ tsp.	7 mL
Large egg, beaten	1	1
Granulated sugar	1 tsp.	5 mL
Warm water	¼ cup	60 mL
Active dry yeast	1 × ¼ oz.	1 × 8 g
All-purpose flour	2 cups	500 mL
All-purpose flour, approximately	1⅓ cups	325 mL
COATING		
Butter or hard margarine	½ cup	125 mL
Granulated sugar	1 cup	250 mL
Ground cinnamon	1 tbsp.	15 mL

Scald milk in saucepan. Remove from heat.

Add next 4 ingredients. Stir to melt butter and dissolve sugar. Cool to lukewarm.

Add beaten egg.

Stir second amount of sugar in warm water in small bowl. Sprinkle yeast over top. Let stand 10 minutes. Stir to dissolve yeast. Add to egg mixture. Pour into large bowl.

Add first amount of flour. Beat until smooth.

Work in enough remaining flour until dough pulls away from sides of bowl. Turn out onto floured surface. Knead about 5 minutes until smooth and elastic. Place in greased bowl, turning once to grease top. Cover with tea towel. Let stand in oven with light on and door closed for about 1 hour until doubled in bulk. Punch dough down. Divide into 2 equal portions. Shape each into a rope. Mark each rope into 12 equal pieces and cut. Roll into balls. Place in greased muffin cups. Cover with tea towel. Let stand in oven with light on and door closed for about 30 minutes until doubled in size. Bake in 375°F (190°C) oven for 15 to 20 minutes until light brown in color. Turn out onto racks to cool.

(continued on next page)

Coating: Melt butter in small saucepan.

Mix sugar and cinnamon in bag or bowl. Dip puffs in butter and shake in bag or set in bowl and spoon sugar mixture over top. Makes 24.

Pictured on cover.

AIR BUNS

Extremely light and airy. Very tasty.

Hot water	**4 cups**	**1 L**
Butter or hard margarine, cut up	**½ cup**	**125 mL**
Granulated sugar	**½ cup**	**125 mL**
White vinegar	**1 tbsp.**	**15 mL**
Salt	**1 tsp.**	**5 mL**
All-purpose flour	**4 cups**	**1 L**
Instant yeast	**1 × ¼ oz.**	**1 × 8 g**
All-purpose flour, approximately	**5¾ cups**	**1.4 L**
Butter or hard margarine, softened, for brushing tops	**2 tbsp.**	**30 mL**

Measure first 5 ingredients into large bowl. Stir to melt butter. Cool to lukewarm.

Combine first amount of flour and yeast in small bowl. Beat slowly into wet ingredients. Beat until smooth.

Work in enough remaining flour until dough pulls away from sides of bowl. Place in greased bowl, turning once to grease top. Cover with tea towel. Let stand in oven with light on and door closed for 1 to 1½ hours until doubled in bulk. Punch dough down. Cover with tea towel. Let stand in oven with light on and door closed for 1 hour. Punch dough down. Shape into 30 egg-size balls. Place on greased baking sheets 2 inches (5 cm) apart. Cover with tea towel. Let stand in oven with light on and door closed for 3 hours. Bake in 350°F (175°C) oven for about 20 minutes until golden brown. Turn out onto racks to cool.

Brush warm tops with butter. Makes 30.

CINNAMON BUNS

Take your pick of variations. The pan buns make nice hot dog or hamburger buns.

Granulated sugar	½ cup	125 mL
Warm water	3 cups	675 mL
Active dry yeast	2 x ¼ oz.	2 x 8 g
Large eggs	2	2
Cooking oil	½ cup	125 mL
Salt	1 tsp.	5 mL
All-purpose flour, approximately	9 cups	2 L
FILLING		
Butter or hard margarine, softened	½ cup	125 mL
Brown sugar, packed	1 cup	250 mL
Ground cinnamon	1 tbsp.	15 mL
ICING		
Icing (confectioner's) sugar	1½ cups	350 mL
Butter or hard margarine, softened	¼ cup	60 mL
Milk or water	3 tbsp.	50 mL
Vanilla	½ tsp.	2 mL

Stir sugar in warm water in large bowl. Sprinkle yeast over top. Let stand 10 minutes. Stir to dissolve yeast.

Mix in eggs, cooking oil and salt. Work in enough flour until dough pulls away from sides of bowl. Turn out onto floured surface. Knead 8 to 10 minutes until smooth and elastic. Divide dough into 4 equal parts. Roll 1 part at a time ¼ inch (6 mm) thick into 9 x 12 inch (22 x 30 cm) rectangle.

Filling: Spread each rectangle with ¼ amount of butter, ¼ amount of brown sugar, and sprinkle with ¼ amount of cinnamon. Roll each rectangle up from long side. Cut into 1 inch (2.5 cm) slices. Place cut side down in greased 9 x 13 inch (22 x 33 cm) pan ¼ inch (6 mm) apart. Cover with tea towel. Let stand in oven with light on and door closed for about 1 hour until doubled in size. Bake in 375°F (190°C) oven for about 20 minutes. Turn out right side up on rack.

Icing: Beat all ingredients together in bowl adding more icing sugar or milk to make a thin glaze. Spoon over warm buns. Makes 48 buns.

(continued on next page)

STICKY CINNAMON BUNS

Brown sugar, packed	1⅓ cups	325 mL
Butter or hard margarine	1 cup	250 mL
Corn syrup	1½ tbsp.	25 mL
Ground cinnamon	1 tbsp.	15 mL
Pecans (optional)	1¼ cups	300 mL

Before cutting Cinnamon Buns, page 50 into 1 inch (2.5 cm) slices, heat and stir above ingredients in saucepan until mixture starts to boil. Boil for 30 seconds. Pour into two 9 x 13 inch (22 x 33 cm) pans. Scatter pecans over hot mixture. Arrange Cinnamon Buns over top, cut side down. Cover with tea towel. Let stand in oven with light on and door closed for about 45 minutes until doubled in size. Bake in 350°F (175°C) oven for 25 to 30 minutes. Turn out onto sheets of foil. Do not ice. Cool slightly before serving.

Pictured on cover.

PAN BUNS: Omit Filling and Icing from Cinnamon Bun recipe. Cut off egg-size pieces of dough. Shape into 48 buns. Place in 2 greased 9 x 13 inch (22 x 33 cm) pans close together. Cover with tea towel. Let stand in oven with light on and door closed for about 1¼ hours until doubled in size. Bake in 375°F (190°C) oven for about 20 minutes. Turn out onto rack to cool. Brush warm tops with butter or hard margarine, softened. Makes 48 buns.

BUTTERSCOTCH BUNS: Simply omit cinnamon.

HAMBURGER BUNS: Make tennis ball size, 4 oz. (152 g). Flatten slightly with your hand. Place on baking sheet 2 inches (5 cm) apart to bake.

HOT DOG BUNS: Make tennis ball size, 4 oz (152 g). Shape into long bun about 5 to 6 inches (12 to 15 cm) long and about 1¼ inches (3 cm) wide. Arrange on baking sheet 2 inches (5 cm) apart to bake.

Paré Pointer

A skeleton is a woman who went on a diet and forgot to say "when".

ITALIAN BREAD CRUMBS

Mild herb taste with a light Romano flavor. Use to coat chicken pieces before baking.

Sliced bread loaf, stale or fresh, cut into narrow strips	1	1
Romano cheese	1 cup	250 mL
Parsley flakes	1 tsp.	5 mL
Sweet basil	1 tsp.	5 mL
Whole oregano	1 tsp.	5 mL
Celery salt	1 tsp.	5 mL
Pepper	¼ tsp.	1 mL
Garlic powder	¼ tsp.	1 mL

Spread bread strips out on ungreased baking sheets. Dry in 250°F (120°C) oven for about 1 hour until crisp. Run through grinder, blender, food processor or roll with rolling pin. If you roll bread between 2 tea towels, it won't slip around and will be much easier to crush.

Stir in remaining ingredients. Store in plastic bag. Makes 3½ cups (875 mL) dry bread crumbs.

BREAD CRUMBS: Omit last 7 ingredients.

FRESH BREAD CRUMBS: Toss dry crumbs as you add a bit of water now and then until moist.

1. Beginner's Croissants, page 33
2. English Muffins, page 77
3. Brioche, page 42
4. Two-Tone Loaf, page 40
5. Easter Egg Bread, page 38
6. Apple Kuchen, page 37
7. Streusel Coffee Cake, page 39
8. Panettone, page 32
9. Danish Pastry, page 45
10. Butterhorns, page 46

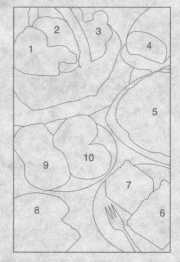

Basket Courtesy Of:
Sissy Walker's Country Interiors
Platter Courtesy Of:
Eaton's China Dept.

Flatware Courtesy Of:
Le Gnome
Plates & Linen Courtesy Of:
La Cache

Glass Tabletop Courtesy Of:
IKEA
Pitcher & Blanket Courtesy Of:
Chintz & Company

KOO-guhl-hoff is a coffee cake made with yeast. It is tasty without being sweet.

Granulated sugar	1 tsp.	5 mL
Warm water	²/₃ cup	150 mL
Active dry yeast	1 x ¹/₄ oz.	1 x 8 g
Butter or hard margarine, softened	¹/₄ cup	60 mL
Granulated sugar	¹/₂ cup	125 mL
Large eggs	2	2
Salt	¹/₂ tsp.	2 mL
All-purpose flour	1 cup	250 mL
All-purpose flour	1¹/₂ cups	375 mL
Raisins	¹/₂ cup	125 mL
Grated lemon rind	2 tsp.	10 mL
Ground almonds (powdery)	2 tbsp.	30 mL

Icing (confectioner's) sugar, sprinkle

Stir first amount of sugar in warm water in small bowl. Sprinkle yeast over top. Let stand 10 minutes. Stir to dissolve yeast.

Cream butter and sugar in medium bowl. Add eggs, 1 at a time, beating well after each addition.

Beat in yeast mixture, salt and first amount of flour. Beat for 4 minutes.

Add next 3 ingredients. Stir well. Cover with greased waxed paper and tea towel. Let stand in oven with light on and door closed for 30 to 45 minutes until doubled in bulk.

Grease 12 cup (2.7 L) bundt pan or 10 inch (25 cm) tube pan. Dust with ground almonds. Punch dough down. Spoon into pan. Cover with greased waxed paper and tea towel. Let stand in oven with light on and door closed for about 1¹/₂ hours until doubled in size. Bake in 350°F (175°C) oven for about 25 minutes. Turn out onto rack to cool.

Sprinkle slightly cooled cake with icing sugar. Serve warm or cool. Makes 1 coffee cake.

SAVARIN

A coffee cake with a creamy filled center and soaked in a rum flavored syrup. SAV-uh-rihn is moist and delicious.

Milk	½ cup	125 mL
Granulated sugar	1 tbsp.	15 mL
Active dry yeast	1 x ¼ oz.	1 x 8 g
All-purpose flour	½ cup	125 mL
All-purpose flour	1½ cups	375 mL
Butter or hard margarine, softened	½ cup	125 mL
Large eggs	4	4
Salt	¼ tsp.	1 mL
SYRUP		
Granulated sugar	1 cup	250 mL
Water	½ cup	125 mL
Rum flavoring	1 tbsp.	15 mL
FILLING		
Whipping cream (or 1 envelope topping)	1 cup	250 mL
Granulated sugar	2 tsp.	10 mL
Vanilla	½ tsp.	2 mL
Rum flavoring	½ tsp.	2 mL

Heat milk in small saucepan until it forms bubbles around the side. Cool to lukewarm. Pour into large bowl.

Stir in first amount of sugar. Sprinkle yeast over top. Let stand 10 minutes. Stir to dissolve yeast.

Mix in first amount of flour. Let stand in oven with light on and door closed for 15 minutes.

Add remaining flour and butter. Beat on low to moisten. Beat in eggs, 1 at a time. Add salt. Beat until smooth. Turn into greased 12 cup (2.7 L) bundt pan. Lay piece of waxed paper over top. Let stand in oven with light on and door closed about 45 minutes until doubled in size. Bake in 350°F (175°C) oven for about 35 minutes. Turn out onto rack. Keep pan aside for next step.

(continued on next page)

Syrup: Boil second amount of sugar and water together for 5 minutes to make syrup.

Add flavoring. Stir. Pour into same bundt pan. Gently lower savarin into syrup in pan. Let stand about 30 minutes until it absorbs all syrup. Transfer to serving plate.

Filling: Beat cream and third amount of sugar in small bowl until stiff. Fold in vanilla and rum flavoring. Fill center of cake with whipped mixture. Makes 1 cake.

Pictured on page 71.

WHOLE WHEAT ROLLS

Light rolls with a good texture. Contains a large proportion of whole wheat flour. You will make these often.

Granulated sugar	1 tsp.	5 mL
Warm water	1¼ cups	300 mL
Active dry yeast	1 × ¼ oz.	1 × 8 g
Large eggs	2	2
Butter or hard margarine, softened	2 tbsp.	30 mL
Mild molasses	3 tbsp.	50 mL
Salt	1 tsp.	5 mL
All-purpose flour	1¾ cups	425 mL
Whole wheat flour, approximately	2¾ cups	675 mL

Stir sugar in warm water in large bowl. Sprinkle yeast over top. Let stand 10 minutes. Stir to dissolve yeast.

Beat in next 5 ingredients in order given. Beat on medium for about 2 minutes until smooth.

Work in enough whole wheat flour until dough pulls away from sides of bowl. Turn out onto floured surface. Knead 8 to 10 minutes until smooth and elastic. Place in greased bowl, turning once to grease top. Cover with tea towel. Let stand in oven with light on and door closed about 1¼ hours until doubled in bulk. Punch dough down. Cut off egg-size pieces. Shape into buns. Place on greased baking sheet. Cover with tea towel. Let stand in oven with light on and door closed for about 45 minutes until doubled in size. Bake in 400°F (205°C) oven for about 12 minutes. Turn out onto racks to cool. Makes 1½ dozen.

ORANGE ROLLS

Lots of orange tang. Sweet and delicious.

Milk	1 cup	225 mL
Granulated sugar	½ cup	125 mL
Butter or hard margarine	¼ cup	60 mL
Salt	¾ tsp.	4 mL
Active dry yeast	1 x ¼ oz.	1 x 8 g
All-purpose flour	2 cups	450 mL
Eggs	3	3
All-purpose flour, approximately	2 cups	500 mL
FILLING		
Grated rind of 1 orange		
Granulated sugar	½ cup	125 mL
Butter or hard margarine, softened	½ cup	125 mL
GLAZE		
Icing (confectioner's) sugar	2 cups	450 mL
Prepared orange juice	¼ cup	60 mL

Heat milk to boiling point in small saucepan. Pour into large bowl.

Stir in sugar, butter and salt. Cool to lukewarm.

Sprinkle yeast over top. Let stand 10 minutes. Stir to dissolve yeast.

Add first amount of flour and eggs. Beat well.

Add remaining flour. Stir. Place in greased bowl, turning to grease entire ball of dough. Cover with damp tea towel. Let stand in oven with light on and door closed about 2 hours until doubled in bulk. Punch dough down. Cut into 2 equal portions. Roll each into 8 x 12 inch (20 x 30 cm) rectangle.

Filling: Mix orange rind, sugar and butter together in small bowl. Stir well. Spread ½ on each rectangle. Roll up starting from long side. Cut into 1½ inch (3.7 cm) slices. Place about 2 inches (5 cm) apart on greased baking sheet. Cover with tea towel. Let stand in oven with light on and door closed about 30 minutes. Bake in 375°F (190°C) oven for 20 minutes. Remove to racks to cool.

Glaze: Stir icing sugar and orange juice together in small bowl. Drizzle over cooled rolls. Makes 16 rolls.

Pictured on page 71.

Neat, round, dark buns with the odd raisin sticking out here and there.

Rye flour	1½ cups	375 mL
All-purpose flour	½ cup	125 mL
Cocoa	2 tbsp.	30 mL
Brown sugar, packed	2 tbsp.	30 mL
Instant coffee granules	1 tsp.	5 mL
Salt	1½ tsp.	7 mL
Instant yeast	1 x ¼ oz.	1 x 8 g
Warm milk	1¼ cups	300 mL
Butter or hard margarine	¼ cup	60 mL
Dark cooking molasses	2 tbsp.	30 mL
Dark raisins	1 cup	250 mL
All-purpose flour, approximately	1¾ cups	425 mL
TOPPING		
Egg white (large)	1	1
Water	1 tbsp.	15 mL

Measure first 7 ingredients into large bowl. Stir.

Combine next 3 ingredients in small bowl. Stir. Add to yeast mixture. Beat until smooth.

Stir in raisins and enough remaining flour until dough pulls away from sides of bowl. Turn out onto floured surface. Knead 8 to 10 minutes until smooth and elastic. Cover with tea towel. Let stand in oven with light on and door closed for 15 minutes. Punch dough down. Shape into egg-size buns. Arrange on greased baking tray 2 inches (5 cm) apart. Cover with tea towel. Let stand in oven with light on and door closed for about 1½ hours until doubled in size.

Topping: Beat egg white and water with fork in small bowl. Brush over buns. Bake in 350°F (175°C) oven for about 25 minutes. Turn out onto racks to cool. Makes 16.

Pictured on cover.

DARK ROLLS

Many different ingredients contribute to the delicious taste in these.

Rolled oats (not instant)	¹/₂ cup	125 mL
All-bran cereal (100%)	¹/₂ cup	125 mL
Whole wheat flour	1 cup	250 mL
Butter or hard margarine	6 tbsp.	100 mL
Mild molasses	3 tbsp.	50 mL
Brown sugar, packed	2 tbsp.	30 mL
Salt	2 tsp.	10 mL
Boiling water	1¹/₂ cups	375 mL
Granulated sugar	2 tsp.	10 mL
Warm water	¹/₂ cup	125 mL
Active dry yeast	2 x ¹/₄ oz.	2 x 8 g
All-purpose flour, approximately	4¹/₂ cups	1.1 L

Measure first 7 ingredients into large bowl. Stir.

Add boiling water. Stir well. Cool to lukewarm.

Stir sugar into warm water in small bowl. Sprinkle yeast over top. Let stand 10 minutes. Stir to dissolve yeast. Add to first mixture in large bowl. Mix.

Work in enough remaining flour until dough pulls away from sides of bowl. Turn out onto floured surface. Knead 3 to 4 minutes. Place in greased bowl, turning once to grease top. Cover with tea towel. Let stand in oven with light on and door closed for about 1 hour until doubled in bulk. Punch dough down. Cut into 24 pieces. Shape into buns. Arrange on greased baking sheet about 1 inch (2.5 cm) apart. Cover with tea towel. Let stand in oven with light on and door closed for about 45 minutes until doubled in size. Bake in 375°F (190°C) oven for about 15 minutes. Turn out onto racks to cool. Makes 24 rolls.

Variation: After cutting dough into 24 pieces, divide each piece into 3 equal parts. Roll each part into 5 to 7 inch (12 to 18 cm) rope. Pinch 3 ends together. Braid on greased baking sheet. Repeat with remaining pieces. Proceed as above. Makes 24 braids.

Pictured on cover.

Paré Pointer

The hunted criminal sawed the legs off his bed because he was advised to lie low for awhile.

Just excellent. Tender and light.

Granulated sugar	1 tsp.	5 mL
Warm water	½ cup	125 mL
Active dry yeast	1 x ¼ oz.	1 x 8 g
Milk	1 cup	250 mL
Butter or hard margarine, cut up	¾ cup	175 mL
Leftover mashed potatoes	1¼ cups	300 mL
Granulated sugar	½ cup	125 mL
Salt	2 tsp.	10 mL
All-purpose flour	2 cups	500 mL
Large eggs, beaten	2	2
All-purpose flour, approximately	6½ cups	1.6 L

Stir sugar in warm water in small bowl. Sprinkle yeast over top. Let stand 10 minutes. Stir to dissolve yeast.

Heat and stir milk, butter and potato in saucepan until butter melts and mixture is warm. Pour into large bowl. Add yeast mixture.

Add next 4 ingredients. Beat well until smooth. Cover with greased waxed paper. Let stand in oven with light on and door closed for 2 hours.

Work in enough remaining flour until dough pulls away from sides of bowl. Place in greased bowl, turning once to grease top. Cover with tea towel. Let stand in oven with light on and door closed for about 1 hour until doubled in bulk. Punch dough down. Divide dough into 3 equal portions. Roll each portion out to a 12 inch (30 cm) circle. Cut into 12 wedges. Roll up each wedge beginning at wide end. Place point side down on greased baking sheet about 2 inches (5 cm) apart. Turn ends inward to make it curved. Cover with tea towel. Let stand in oven with light on and door closed for about 30 minutes until nearly doubled in size. Bake in 400°F (205°C) oven for about 15 minutes until golden. Turn out onto racks to cool. Makes 3 dozen.

Pictured on page 71.

While robbing a house, have a bath so you can make a clean getaway.

OVERNIGHT BREAKFAST BUNS

Divide dough into thirds and make 1 dozen of each. What a breakfast!

Granulated sugar	1 tsp.	5 mL
Warm water	1/4 cup	60 mL
Active dry yeast	1 x 1/4 oz.	1 x 8 g
Boiling water	2³/4 cups	675 mL
Granulated sugar	1 cup	250 mL
Butter or hard margarine	1/2 cup	125 mL
Salt	1 tbsp.	15 mL
All-purpose flour, approximately	8 cups	2 L

Begin at 5:00 p.m. Stir first amount of sugar in warm water in small bowl. Sprinkle yeast over top. Let stand 10 minutes. Stir to dissolve yeast.

Pour boiling water into large bowl. Stir in second amount of sugar, butter and salt until sugar is dissolved and butter is melted. Cool to lukewarm. Add yeast mixture.

Beat in about 1/4 of the flour. Work in enough remaining flour until dough pulls away from sides of bowl. Place in greased bowl, turning once to grease top. Cover with tea towel. Let stand on counter until 7:00 p.m. Punch dough down. Cover with tea towel. Let stand on counter until 10:00 p.m. Punch dough down. Divide into 36 egg-size pieces. Shape into buns. Arrange on greased baking sheets. Cover with tea towel. Let stand on kitchen counter until morning. Bake in 375°F (190°C) oven for 15 to 20 minutes. Makes 3 dozen.

Pictured on page 71.

OVERNIGHT CINNAMON BUNS: Divide dough into thirds. Roll dough into 14 inch (35 cm) square. Spread each square with 1/2 cup (125 mL) butter or hard margarine, softened. Sprinkle with 1 cup (250 mL) brown sugar and 2 tbsp. (30 mL) cinnamon. Roll up from long side and cut each roll into 12. Proceed as above. Makes 3 dozen cinnamon buns.

Pictured on page 71.

OVERNIGHT CLOVERLEAF ROLLS: Divide dough into thirds. Divide each ball into 12 pieces. Divide each piece into 3 balls. Place 3 balls in each of 12 muffin cups. Proceed as above. Makes 3 dozen rolls.

Slightly sweet bread with a buttery flavor.

Milk	2 cups	500 mL
Butter or hard margarine	3 tbsp.	50 mL
Granulated sugar	2 tbsp.	30 mL
Salt	1 tsp.	5 mL
Granulated sugar	1 tsp.	5 mL
Warm water	1/4 cup	60 mL
Active dry yeast	1 x 1/4 oz.	1 x 8 g
All-purpose flour	3 cups	750 mL
All-purpose flour, approximately	2 1/2 cups	625 mL
Butter or hard margarine, melted	2 tbsp.	30 mL

Combine milk, butter, first amount of sugar and salt in saucepan. Heat and stir to scald milk. Cool to lukewarm.

Stir second amount of sugar in warm water in small bowl. Sprinkle yeast over top. Let stand 10 minutes. Stir to dissolve yeast. Pour lukewarm milk mixture into large bowl. Add yeast mixture. Stir.

Add first amount of flour. Beat well.

Work in enough remaining flour until dough pulls away from sides of bowl. Turn out onto floured surface. Knead 7 to 8 minutes until smooth and elastic. Place in greased bowl, turning once to grease top. Cover with tea towel. Let stand in oven with light on and door closed for about 1 1/2 hours until doubled in bulk. Punch dough down.

Roll out dough 1/4 to 1/3 inch (6 to 8 mm) thick. Cut in 3 inch (7.5 cm) circles. Pull into slightly oblong shape. Butter 1/2 of top side. Make crease with dull edge of knife in center crosswise. Fold one half over buttered half. Gently press ends together. Do not flatten. Arrange on greased baking sheet 1/2 inch (12 mm) apart. Cover with tea towel. Let stand in oven with light on and door closed about 45 minutes until almost doubled in size. Bake in 400°F (205°C) oven for 10 to 15 minutes. Remove to racks to cool. Makes 3 dozen.

Pictured on page 71.

CHEESE BUNS: Add 2 cups (500 mL) grated sharp Cheddar cheese with first amount of flour. Shape into egg-size buns. Sprinkle each bun with a few shreds of cheese before baking. Bake in 375°F (190°C) oven for 15 to 20 minutes. Cool on racks. Makes 2 dozen.

HOT CROSS BUNS

Not just at Easter—great all year round!

Milk, scalded and cooled to lukewarm	2 cups	500 mL
Granulated sugar	2 tsp.	10 mL
Warm water	1/2 cup	125 mL
Active dry yeast	2 x 1/4 oz.	2 x 8 g
All-purpose flour	3 cups	750 mL
Butter or hard margarine, softened	1/2 cup	125 mL
Granulated sugar	3/4 cup	175 mL
Large eggs	2	2
Salt	1 tsp.	5 mL
Ground cinnamon	1 tsp.	5 mL
Ground nutmeg	1/8 tsp.	0.5 mL
Ground cloves	1/8 tsp.	0.5 mL
Currants or raisins	1 cup	250 mL
All-purpose flour, approximately	3 1/2 cups	875 mL
Butter or hard margarine, softened, for brushing tops	2 tsp.	10 mL
GLAZE		
Icing (confectioner's) sugar	1 cup	250 mL
Milk or water	1 tbsp.	15 mL
Vanilla	1/4 tsp.	1 mL

Pour warm milk into large bowl.

Stir first amount of sugar in warm water in small bowl. Sprinkle yeast over top. Let stand 10 minutes. Stir to dissolve yeast. Add to milk. Stir.

Beat in first amount of flour until very smooth. Cover with greased waxed paper and tea towel. Let stand in oven with light on and door closed for about 50 minutes until bubbly and light.

Cream butter and second amount of sugar in another bowl. Beat in eggs 1 at a time. Add next 5 ingredients. Stir. Add to flour mixture. Stir.

(continued on next page)

Work in enough remaining flour until dough pulls away from sides of bowl. Turn out onto floured surface. Knead about 5 minutes until smooth and elastic. Place dough in greased bowl, turning once to grease top. Cover with tea towel. Let stand in oven with light on and door closed for about 1 hour until doubled in bulk. Punch dough down. Divide into 3 equal portions. Divide each portion into 12 pieces. Shape into buns. Arrange in 3 greased 8 x 8 inch (20 x 20 cm) pans. Cover with tea towel. Let stand in oven with light on and door closed for about 1 hour until doubled in size. Cut with scissors or slash with knife or razor blade to make a cross on top $\frac{1}{8}$ inch (3 mm) deep. Bake in 375°F (190°C) oven for 12 to 15 minutes. Turn out onto racks to cool.

Brush warm tops with butter. Continue to cool.

Glaze: Mix all 3 ingredients together to make a barely pourable glaze. Drizzle or pipe over slashes in cooled buns. Makes 36.

Pictured on page 71.

TWO-HOUR BUNS

Makes a nice big batch—and yet so quick.

All-purpose flour	4 cups	900 mL
Instant yeast	2 x ¼ oz.	2 x 8 g
Large eggs	2	2
Cooking oil	½ cup	125 mL
Water	3 cups	675 mL
Salt	1 tsp.	5 mL
All-purpose flour, approximately	5 cups	1.1 L
Butter or hard margarine, softened, for brushing tops	2 tsp.	10 mL

Combine flour and yeast in large bowl.

Beat eggs, cooking oil and water together in separate bowl. Add to flour mixture. Add salt. Mix well.

Work in enough remaining flour until dough pulls away from sides of bowl. Cover with tea towel. Let stand in oven with light on and door closed for 15 minutes. Punch dough down. Shape into 48 egg-size buns. Place in 2 greased 9 x 13 inch (22 x 33 cm) pans. Cover with tea towel. Let stand in oven with light on and door closed for about 45 minutes until doubled in size. Bake in 350°F (175°C) oven for 25 to 30 minutes. Turn out onto racks to cool.

Brush warm tops with butter. Makes 48 buns.

Pictured on page 71.

SOFT PRETZELS

Salted or seeded, these are a wonderful snack.

Granulated sugar	**1 tsp.**	**5 mL**
Warm water	**¼ cup**	**60 mL**
Active dry yeast	**1 × ¼ oz.**	**1 × 8 g**
Warm water	**1½ cups**	**375 mL**
All-purpose flour	**4½ cups**	**1 L**
Salt	**½ tsp.**	**2 mL**
TOPPING		
Egg white (large)	**1**	**1**
Water	**1 tbsp.**	**15 mL**
Coarse salt		
Sesame seeds		

Stir sugar into first amount of warm water in small bowl. Sprinkle yeast over top. Let stand for 10 minutes. Stir to dissolve yeast.

Combine second amount of warm water, flour and salt in large bowl. Add yeast mixture. Add a bit more flour if needed so dough isn't too sticky. Turn out onto floured surface. Knead 8 to 10 minutes until smooth and elastic. Place in greased bowl, turning once to grease top. Cover with tea towel. Let stand in oven with light on and door closed about 45 minutes until doubled in bulk. Punch dough down. Roll into log. Mark off into 12 portions. Cut. Roll each portion into ½ inch (12 mm) thick rope. Shape each rope into pretzel on greased baking sheets.

Beat egg white and water with fork in small bowl. Brush over pretzels.

Sprinkle some pretzels with coarse salt and some with sesame seeds. Bake in 450°F (230°C) oven for about 15 minutes. Turn out onto racks to cool. Makes 12.

Pictured on cover.

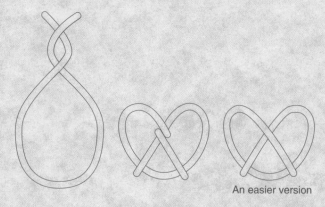

An easier version

Now this is a real bun. Seeds inside and on top. Great to sink your teeth into.

All-purpose flour	1 cup	250 mL
Whole wheat flour	1 cup	250 mL
Cracked wheat	1 cup	250 mL
Salt	1 tsp.	5 mL
Sunflower seeds	1 cup	250 mL
Sesame seeds	2 tbsp.	30 mL
Brown sugar, packed	1/4 cup	60 mL
Instant yeast	1 x 1/4 oz.	1 x 8 g
Warm water	1 1/3 cups	325 mL
Cooking oil	1/4 cup	60 mL
All-purpose flour, approximately	1 1/4 cups	300 mL
TOPPING		
Large egg	1	1
Water	1 tbsp.	15 mL
Sunflower seeds	1 tbsp.	15 mL
Sesame seeds	1 tsp.	5 mL
Poppy seeds	1 tsp.	5 mL
Cracked wheat	2 tsp.	10 mL

Stir first 8 ingredients together in large bowl.

Add warm water and cooking oil. Mix.

Work in enough remaining flour until dough pulls away from sides of bowl. Turn out onto floured surface. Knead about 4 minutes. Place in greased bowl, turning once to grease top. Cover with tea towel. Let stand in oven with light on and door closed for about 1½ hours until doubled in bulk. Punch dough down. Cut dough into egg-size pieces. Shape into buns. Set aside momentarily.

Topping: Beat egg and water with fork in small bowl.

Stir next 4 ingredients together in another bowl. Brush top of each bun with egg wash, dip in seeds and arrange on greased baking sheet at least 1 inch (2.5 cm) apart. Cover with tea towel. Let stand in oven with light on and door closed for about 45 minutes until doubled in size. Bake in 375°F (190°C) oven for about 20 minutes. Turn out onto racks to cool. Makes 16.

Pictured on cover.

BAGELS

Real gems! Cut in half and toast, serve with flavored cream cheese or broil each half with Cheddar cheese. The possibilities are endless.

Granulated sugar	1 tsp.	5 mL
Warm water	¾ cup	175 mL
Active dry yeast	1 × ¼ oz.	1 × 8 g
Large eggs	2	2
Cooking oil	2 tbsp.	30 mL
All-purpose flour	2 cups	500 mL
Granulated sugar	1 tbsp.	15 mL
Salt	1¾ tsp.	9 mL
All-purpose flour, approximately	1½ cups	375 mL
POACHING LIQUID		
Water	4 quarts	4 L
Granulated sugar	2 tbsp.	30 mL
TOPPING		
Large egg, beaten	1	1
Sesame seeds or poppy seeds, to coat tops		

Stir first amount of sugar in warm water in large bowl. Sprinkle yeast over top. Let stand 10 minutes. Stir to dissolve yeast.

Whisk in eggs and cooking oil. Beat in first amount of flour, second amount of sugar and salt until smooth.

Work in enough remaining flour to make a soft dough. Turn out onto floured surface. Knead 8 to 10 minutes until dough is smooth and elastic. Place in greased bowl, turning once to grease top. Cover with tea towel. Let stand in oven with light on and door closed for 1 to 1½ hours until doubled in bulk. Punch dough down. Divide into 12 equal portions. Roll each portion into 10 inch (25 cm) rope. Cover remaining portions with damp tea towel while rolling and shaping each rope. Bring the ends of rope together, overlapping slightly. Pinch end to firmly seal. Place on floured baking sheet. Cover with tea towel. Let stand in oven with light on and door closed for 15 minutes.

(continued on next page)

Poaching liquid: Bring water to a boil in large saucepan. Add sugar. Reduce heat to medium to keep water at a slow boil. Slip bagels into water, 3 or 4 at a time. Poach for 1 minute. Turn. Poach 1 minute. Remove bagels to well-greased baking sheet.

Topping: Brush egg over top of each bagel. Sprinkle with sesame or poppy seeds. Bake in 400°F (205°C) oven for 20 to 25 minutes or until golden brown. Place on racks to cool. Makes 12 bagels.

Pictured on page 125.

WHOLE WHEAT BAGELS: Use half all-purpose flour and half whole wheat flour. Replace 2 tbsp. (30 mL) liquid with 1 tbsp. (15 mL) each of honey and mild molasses.

Pictured on cover and on page 125.

RAISIN BAGELS: Add 1 tbsp. (15 mL) ground cinnamon and ⅓ cup (75 mL) dark raisins with dry ingredients.

FLAVORED CREAM CHEESE SPREAD

Serve with Bagels, page 68, Pumpernickel, page 121 or any whole wheat or rye breads.

Cream cheese, softened	**4 oz**	**125 g**
FLAVORINGS		
Garlic Powder	**¼ tsp.**	**1 mL**
Grated parmesan cheese	**2 tbsp.**	**30 mL**
Honey	**¼ cup**	**60 mL**
Orange marmalade	**¼ cup**	**60 mL**
Maple-flavored syrup	**1 tbsp.**	**15 mL**
Frozen concentrated orange juice	**1 tbsp.**	**15 mL**

Beat cream cheese in bowl until quite softened.

Flavorings: Add one of the flavorings. Mix well. Makes ½ cup (125 mL).

Paré Pointer

Don't blame mathematics for your divorce just because your wife put two and two together.

CROUTONS

Toss in with your favorite salad or drop a spoonful in a hot bowl of soup.

Stale bread slices	**8**	**8**
Butter or hard margarine, softened	**½ cup**	**125 mL**

Lay bread on counter. Spread both sides lightly with butter. Stack slices 2 or 4 high. Cut into ½ inch (12 mm) cubes. Arrange on ungreased baking sheet. Bake in 300°F (150°C) oven for 25 to 30 minutes until golden brown. Stir occasionally while browning. If you prefer, you can stir-fry these to brown. Makes about 4 cups.

PARMESAN CROUTONS: Sprinkle both sides of buttered bread with grated Parmesan. Run knife over after each sprinkle.

SEASONED CROUTONS: Mix ½ tsp. (2 mL) seasoned salt with butter before buttering bread.

GARLIC CROUTONS: Mix ½ tsp. (2 mL) garlic salt with butter before buttering bread.

HERB CROUTONS: Mix ¼ tsp. (1 mL) each of garlic powder, whole oregano, thyme and sweet basil with butter before buttering bread.

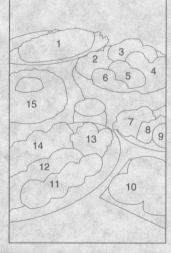

Platters Courtesy Of:
La Cache

Pot Courtesy Of:
IKEA

Linen Courtesy Of:
Enchanted Kitchen

Flowers Courtesy Of:
Eaton's Housewares Dept.

Wood Tabletop Courtesy Of:
IKEA

Neat looking rolls. Easy to break off the three knobs, one at a time.

Boiling water	2½ cups	625 mL
Butter or hard margarine	¼ cup	60 mL
Granulated sugar	1 tbsp.	15 mL
Salt	2 tsp.	10 mL
Granulated sugar	2 tsp.	10 mL
Warm water	½ cup	125 mL
Active dry yeast	1 × ¼ oz.	1 × 8 g
All-purpose flour	4 cups	1 L
All-purpose flour, approximately	5½ cups	1.3 L
Butter or hard margarine, melted	2-3 tbsp.	30-50 mL

Measure first 4 ingredients into large bowl. Stir to melt butter. Cool to lukewarm.

Stir second amount of sugar in warm water in small bowl. Sprinkle yeast over top. Let stand 10 minutes. Stir to dissolve yeast. Add to mixture in large bowl.

Add first amount of flour. Beat until smooth.

Work in enough remaining flour until dough pulls away from sides of bowl. Place in greased bowl, turning once to grease top. Cover with greased waxed paper and tea towel. Let stand in oven with light on and door closed about 1½ hours until doubled in bulk. Punch dough down. Divide dough into 4 equal portions. Divide each of 4 portions in half, making 8 pieces. Roll each into a log 6 inches (15 cm) long. Divide each log into 3 pieces. Divide each of the 3 pieces into 6 balls. Put 3 balls each into greased muffin cup.

Brush tops with melted butter. Cover with greased waxed paper and tea towel. Let stand in oven with light on and door closed about 45 minutes until doubled in size. Bake in 400°F (205°C) oven for about 15 minutes until golden. Turn out onto racks to cool. Makes 48 rolls.

Pictured on cover.

STOLLEN

A Christmas yeast cake. Fruity. Just meant for coffee breaks.

Raisins	½ cup	125 mL
Currants	¼ cup	60 mL
Cut mixed glazed fruit, finely cut	1 cup	250 mL
Cut citron peel	⅓ cup	75 mL
Grated rind of 1 lemon		
Slivered almonds	½ cup	125 mL
All-purpose flour	¼ cup	60 mL
All-purpose flour	2 cups	500 mL
Granulated sugar	½ cup	125 mL
Salt	1½ tsp.	7 mL
Instant yeast	2 × ¼ oz.	2 × 8 g
Very warm milk (warm enough to melt butter)	1¼ cups	300 mL
Butter or hard margarine	½ cup	125 mL
Vanilla	1 tsp.	5 mL
Ground cardamom	¼ tsp.	1 mL
All-purpose flour, approximately	2½ cups	625 mL

TOPPING

Icing (confectioner's) sugar, sprinkle, or Glaze, page 64		
Chopped glazed cherries or chopped walnuts	¼ cup	60 mL

Combine first 7 ingredients in bowl. Stir to coat with flour. Set aside.

Stir second amount of flour, sugar, salt and yeast in large bowl.

Add warm milk, butter, vanilla and cardamom. Beat until smooth. Add fruit mixture.

Work in enough remaining flour until dough pulls away from sides of bowl. Cover with tea towel. Let stand in oven with light on and door closed about 2 hours until doubled in bulk. Divide dough in half. Roll each half out on floured surface into 8 × 12 inch (20 × 30 cm) rectangle. Fold over lengthwise keeping top edge 1 inch (2.5 cm) back from edge of bottom. Place on greased baking sheets. Cover with tea towel. Let stand in oven with light on and door closed for about 1 hour until almost doubled in size. Bake in 375°F (190°C) oven for about 15 minutes. Remove to racks to cool. Makes 2 loaves.

Topping: Sift icing sugar over slightly cooled tops or drizzle with glaze. Sprinkle with cherries or nuts.

Pictured on page 71.

A medium-size delicate bun to serve at a salad luncheon, with tea, as an open face sandwich or with any meal.

Large eggs	2	2
Granulated sugar	¼ cup	60 mL
Salt	1 tsp.	5 mL
Cooking oil	½ cup	125 mL
Water	1 cup	250 mL
Milk	1 cup	250 mL
Granulated sugar	1 tsp.	5 mL
Warm water	½ cup	125 mL
Active dry yeast	1 x ¼ oz.	1 x 8 g
All-purpose flour, approximately	8¼ cups	2 L

Beat eggs in large bowl. Beat in first amount of sugar and salt. Add cooking oil, first amount of water and milk. Mix.

Stir second amount of sugar in warm water in small bowl. Sprinkle yeast over top. Let stand 10 minutes. Stir to dissolve yeast. Add to egg mixture. Mix.

Work in enough flour until dough pulls away from sides of bowl. Turn out onto floured surface. Knead 8 to 10 minutes until smooth and elastic. Place in greased bowl, turning once to grease top. Cover with tea towel. Let stand in oven with light on and door closed for about 1½ hours until doubled in bulk. Punch dough down. Divide dough into 36 egg-size pieces. Shape into buns. Arrange on greased baking sheets about 1½ inches (4 cm) apart. Cover with tea towel. Let stand in oven with light on and door closed for about 45 minutes until doubled in size. Bake in 375°F (190°C) oven for about 20 minutes. Makes 3 dozen.

They chased the pigs back and forth through the garden so they could raise mashed potatoes.

COTTAGE WHEAT ROLLS

Colossal rolls especially suited for soups and stews. Can easily be made smaller.

Large eggs	2	2
Brown sugar, packed	$\frac{1}{3}$ cup	75 mL
Creamed cottage cheese	2 cups	500 mL
Cooking oil	2 tbsp.	30 mL
Mild molasses	2 tbsp.	30 mL
Salt	1 tsp.	5 mL
Whole wheat flour	$1\frac{1}{2}$ cups	375 mL
Instant yeast	$2 \times \frac{1}{4}$ oz.	2×8 g
Baking soda	$\frac{1}{2}$ tsp.	2 mL
Whole wheat flour, approximately	$2\frac{3}{4}$ cups	675 mL

Beat eggs in large bowl. Beat in next 5 ingredients in order given.

Add next 3 ingredients. Beat on low to moisten. Beat on high for 3 minutes.

Work in enough remaining flour until dough pulls away from sides of bowl. Turn out onto floured surface. Knead 8 to 10 minutes until smooth and elastic. Place in greased bowl, turning once to grease top. Cover with tea towel. Let stand in oven with light on and door closed for $1\frac{1}{2}$ to 2 hours until doubled in bulk. Punch dough down. Cut dough into 14 pieces for large rolls. Shape into $1\frac{1}{4}$ inch (3 cm) diameter. Place on greased baking sheet 2 inches (5 cm) apart. Cover with tea towel. Let stand in oven with light on and door closed about $1\frac{1}{4}$ hours until doubled in size. Bake in 375°F (190°C) oven for about 12 minutes. Turn out onto racks to cool. Makes 14.

Pictured on page 71.

Loudspeakers have their place, anyplace but home.

So easy to make your own.

Granulated sugar	2 tbsp.	30 mL
Warm water	½ cup	125 mL
Active dry yeast	1 x ¼ oz.	1 x 8 g
Milk	1 cup	250 mL
Butter or hard margarine, softened	3 tbsp.	50 mL
Large egg, beaten	1	1
All-purpose flour	2 cups	500 mL
Salt	1 tsp.	5 mL
Ground ginger	¼ tsp.	1 mL
All-purpose flour, approximately	2¾ cups	675 mL
Cornmeal, sprinkle		

Stir sugar and warm water together in medium bowl. Sprinkle yeast over top. Let stand 10 minutes. Stir to dissolve yeast.

Heat milk and butter in small saucepan until lukewarm. Stir into yeast mixture.

Stir in egg.

Measure first amount of flour, salt and ginger into large bowl. Add yeast mixture. Stir.

Work in enough remaining flour until dough pulls away from sides of bowl. Turn out onto floured surface. Knead 3 to 5 minutes until smooth and elastic. Place in greased bowl, turning once to grease top. Cover with tea towel. Let stand in oven with light on and door closed for about 1 hour until doubled in bulk. Roll dough a scant ½ inch (12 mm) thick on lightly floured surface. Cut into 3½ inch (9 cm) rounds.

Sprinkle cornmeal on working surface. Set each round on cornmeal pressing lightly. Turn and repeat. Grease heavy frying pan or griddle that is heated to medium. Brown circles slowly on both sides, about 8 minutes per side. Pan should not require greasing between batches. Makes 1 dozen.

Pictured on page 53.

WHEAT ENGLISH MUFFINS: Use 2 cups (450 mL) whole wheat flour and approximately 2 cups (450 mL) all-purpose flour.

SOUR CREAM DOUGHNUTS

These rise to the occasion. A "great anytime" snack.

Large eggs	2	2
Granulated sugar	¾ cup	175 mL
Sour cream	¾ cup	175 mL
Sour milk (or 1½ tsp., 7 mL, white vinegar plus milk)	½ cup	125 mL
Vanilla	1½ tsp.	7 mL
All-purpose flour	4 cups	1 L
Baking soda	1 tsp.	5 mL
Ground nutmeg	½ tsp.	2 mL
Ground cinnamon	½ tsp.	2 mL
Salt	½ tsp.	2 mL

Fat, for deep-frying (see Note)

Beat eggs in large bowl until light. Beat in sugar. Add sour cream, sour milk and vanilla. Beat to blend in.

Stir flour, baking soda, nutmeg, cinnamon and salt together in separate bowl. Add to batter. Stir to moisten. Roll scant ½ inch (1 cm) thick. Cut with doughnut cutter.

Deep-fry 2 or 3 at a time in hot 375°F (190°C) fat until browned on both sides. Remove with slotted spoon onto paper towels. Cool. Stand on edge to drain. Makes about 2 dozen.

Pictured on cover.

Note: "Holes" can be deep-fried also.

Pictured on cover.

SUGARED DOUGHNUTS: Pour ¼ cup (60 mL) granulated sugar in bag. Drop in doughnuts, 1 at a time. Shake.

CINNAMON DOUGHNUTS: Place ¼ cup (60 mL) granulated sugar and ¼ tsp (1 mL) ground cinnamon in bag. Shake. Drop in doughnuts 1 at a time. Shake.

Jimmy's grades were under water. His teacher said they were below C level.

Soh-pah-PEE-yah is a favorite Mexican-fried bread. Try dipping in honey to eat.

All-purpose flour	2 cups	500 mL
Dry skim milk powder	1/3 cup	75 mL
Baking powder	2 tsp.	10 mL
Salt	1 tsp.	5 mL
Butter or hard margarine	2 tbsp.	30 mL
Warm milk	1 cup	250 mL

Fat, for deep-frying

Measure flour, skim milk powder, baking powder and salt into medium bowl. Stir.

Add butter. Cut in until mixture is crumbly.

Add milk. Stir to make a ball. Turn out onto floured surface. Knead 8 to 10 times. Cover with tea towel. Let stand on counter 20 to 30 minutes. Roll 1/2 dough at a time as thin as you can on lightly floured surface. Cut into 3 inch (7.5 cm) squares.

Deep-fry 2 or 3 at a time in hot 375°F (190°C) fat, turning and pushing beneath surface of fat as they puff up and brown. Remove with slotted spoon onto paper towel to drain. Makes about 32.

Pictured on page 71.

Paré Pointer

A gram cracker is a metric cookie.

OLIE BOLLEN

Crispy on the outside—like a fritter on the inside.

Warm water	½ cup	125 mL
Granulated sugar	3 tbsp.	50 mL
Active dry yeast	1 x ¼ oz.	1 x 8 g
Eggs, well beaten	2	2
Milk	1½ cups	375 mL
Vanilla	½ tsp.	2 mL
Salt	1 tsp.	5 mL
Raisins	2 cups	500 mL
Cooking apples, peeled and finely diced (McIntosh is good)	2½ cups	625 mL
All-purpose flour	4 cups	1 L

Fat, for deep-frying

Icing (confectioner's) sugar

Stir warm water and sugar together in large bowl. Sprinkle yeast over top. Let stand 10 minutes. Stir to dissolve yeast.

Add next 7 ingredients in order given. Mix. Cover with greased waxed paper and tea towel. Let stand in oven with light on and door closed 1½ hours until doubled in bulk.

Drop by tablespoonful in hot fat 375°F (190°C) to brown. Cool on rack.

Sprinkle with icing sugar when cool. Makes about 48.

Pictured on page 71.

He loves a cigar after a good meal. Apparently he hasn't smoked one at home yet.

Just like the store-bought.

Granulated sugar	¼ cup	60 mL
Butter or hard margarine	1½ tbsp.	25 mL
Salt	1½ tsp.	7 mL
Ground nutmeg	1 tsp.	5 mL
Milk, scalded	¾ cup	175 mL
Large egg, beaten	1	1
Granulated sugar	1 tsp.	5 mL
Warm water	¼ cup	60 mL
Active dry yeast	1 x ¼ oz.	1 x 8 g
All-purpose flour, approximately	3¼ cups	725 mL
Fat, for deep-frying (see Note)		
Icing (confectioner's) sugar	1 cup	250 mL

Combine first 4 ingredients in large bowl. Add scalded milk. Stir. Cool to lukewarm.

Mix in beaten egg.

Stir second amount of sugar in warm water in small bowl. Sprinkle yeast over top. Let stand 10 minutes. Stir to dissolve yeast. Add to batter. Stir.

Work in enough flour until dough pulls away from sides of bowl. Turn out onto floured surface. Knead 8 to 10 minutes until smooth and elastic. Place in greased bowl, turning once to grease top. Cover with tea towel. Let stand in oven with light on and door closed for about 1½ hours until doubled in bulk. Punch dough down. Cover with tea towel. Let stand in oven with light on and door closed for 30 minutes. Roll out ½ inch (12 mm) thick on lightly floured board. Cut with doughnut cutter. Cover with tea towel. Let stand in oven with light on and door closed for about 1 hour until doubled in size.

Deep-fry in hot 375°F (190°C) fat, placing raised side (top side) down until brown. Turn to brown other side. Drain on paper towels.

Dip in icing sugar while hot, if desired. Makes 18 doughnuts.

Pictured on page 71.

Note: "Holes" can be deep-fried also.

CRULLERS: Roll dough ½ inch (12 mm) thick. Cut in 3 x ½ inch (7.5 x 1 cm) strips. Twist and pinch ends together. Cover. Let rise until doubled in size. Deep-fry.

Pictured on page 71.

BEIGNETS: Roll, without pre-rising, ¼ to ½ inch (6 to 12 mm) thick. Cut into 2 inch (5 cm) squares or larger. Deep-fry. Drain. Coat with icing sugar.

Pictured on page 71.

FLOUR TORTILLAS

Very easy to make. Keep some in the freezer for a snack by themselves, or as a quick lunch with a filling.

All-purpose flour	2 cups	500 mL
Baking powder	1 tsp.	5 mL
Salt	1 tsp.	5 mL
Butter or hard margarine	1/4 cup	60 mL
Water	2/3 cup	150 mL

Place flour, baking powder and salt in medium bowl. Cut in butter until crumbly.

Add water. Stir until dough forms a ball. If too dry to form a firm ball, add 1 tbsp. (15 mL) of water at a time until it will. Turn out onto floured surface. Knead 6 to 8 times. Cover with inverted bowl. Let rest 20 minutes. Roll out a portion as thin as you can. Invert 7 inch (18 cm) bowl or 8 inch (20 cm) plate on dough. Cut around edge. Repeat. Place 1 tortilla on medium hot ungreased frying pan. Some dark spots will appear in 15 to 20 seconds. Turn. Brown 15 to 20 seconds on second side until there are some dark spots. Keep warm in tea towel. Cool and wrap air tight to store. Makes 10 to 12.

YEAST FLATBREAD

Nice golden crust with a homey and satisfying taste. Be sure and try both toppings.

Granulated sugar	1 tsp.	5 mL
Warm water	1 1/2 cups	375 mL
Active yeast	1 x 1/4 oz.	1 x 8 g
All-purpose flour	3 cups	750 mL
Salt	1 1/2 tsp.	7 mL
TOPPING		
Cooking oil	1-2 tsp.	5-10 mL
Sesame seeds	1 tbsp.	15 mL
Italian seasoning	1 tbsp.	15 mL

(continued on next page)

Stir sugar in warm water in large bowl. Sprinkle yeast over top. Stir once. Let stand 10 minutes. Stir to dissolve yeast.

Add flour and salt. Beat on low to moisten. Beat on high until smooth. Stir. Turn out onto floured surface. Knead until smooth and elastic. Place in greased bowl, turning once to grease top. Cover with tea towel. Let stand in oven with light on and door closed about 35 minutes until doubled in size. Punch dough down. Divide dough into 2 equal portions. Roll out or pat each portion to 10 inch (25 cm) round circle. Transfer to greased baking sheets.

Topping: Brush tops with cooking oil. Sprinkle 1 round with sesame seeds. Sprinkle 1 round with Italian seasoning. Bake in 400°F (205°C) oven for 20 to 25 minutes until golden. Makes 2 round loaves.

Pictured on page 89.

GRAHAM CRACKERS

Look and taste like the store-bought kind. Delicious.

All-purpose flour	1¼ cups	300 mL
Graham flour (or whole wheat)	1 cup	250 mL
Brown sugar, packed	¼ cup	60 mL
Salt	1 tsp.	5 mL
Baking powder	1 tsp.	5 mL
Baking soda	½ tsp.	2 mL
Butter or hard margarine	¾ cup	175 mL
Warm water	¼ cup	60 mL
Honey	¼ cup	60 mL
Vanilla	1 tsp.	5 mL

Measure first 6 ingredients into medium bowl. Cut in butter until mixture is mealy.

Stir water, honey and vanilla in small bowl until mixed. Pour into flour mixture. Stir to make a ball. Divide dough in half. Roll ½ dough directly on ungreased 10 x 15 inches (25 x 38 cm) baking sheet to ⅛ inch (3 mm) thick. Dust rolling pin with flour as needed. Using ruler, mark off 2 inch (5 cm) squares without cutting through dough. Prick with fork all over in even rows. Bake in 425°F (220°C) oven for 10 to 12 minutes until browned. They will crisp as they cool. Cut on lines. Makes 60 crackers.

Picture on page 89.

LEFSE

A lefse rolling pin really works the best. These make a nutritious snack for the kids.

Milk	2 cups	500 mL
Evaporated skim milk (or cream)	1 cup	250 mL
Butter or hard margarine	1/2 cup	125 mL
Salt	1 tsp.	5 mL
Granulated sugar (optional)	2 tbsp.	30 mL
Potato flakes	3 cups	750 mL
All-purpose flour	1 1/3 cups	325 mL

Heat first 5 ingredients in large saucepan, stirring often, until butter melts. Remove from heat.

Add potato flakes. Whip in until smooth. Cool completely.

Mix flour into potato mixture. Turn out onto well-floured surface. Knead 6 to 8 times. Divide into 20 equal portions. Roll each portion, dusting with flour as needed, as thin as possible. Fry on hot griddle about 1 scant minute until you see brown spots. Turn and fry 1 more scant minute. Makes 20.

Pictured on page 89.

CINNAMON LEFSE: Spread cooled lefse with butter or margarine. Sprinkle with granulated sugar and cinnamon. Fold twice into quarters or roll up like a jelly roll. May be spread with jam instead of sugar and cinnamon.

Pictured on page 89.

NAAN

Soft and chewy. Cut or tear into pieces and serve as a healthy snack for the kids.

Large eggs	2	2
Plain yogurt	1/4 cup	60 mL
Milk	3/4 cup	175 mL
Cooking oil	1/4 cup	60 mL
All-purpose flour	4 cups	1 L
Granulated sugar	1 tbsp.	15 mL
Baking powder	1 tbsp.	15 mL
Baking soda	1/2 tsp.	2 mL
Salt	1 1/2 tsp.	7 mL

(continued on next page)

Beat eggs in large bowl until frothy. Add yogurt, milk and cooking oil. Mix.

Measure remaining ingredients into separate bowl. Stir well. Add to egg mixture. Stir. Turn out onto floured surface. Knead 8 to 10 times until dough is smooth. Cut into 30 pieces about the size of a golf ball. Cover with damp tea towel. Let stand 1 hour. Roll or pat each ball on floured surface into 6 inch (15 cm) circles. Arrange on greased baking sheets. Bake in 450°F (230°C) oven for about 3 to 4 minutes until puffed and browned. Makes 30.

OATMEAL CRACKERS

Crunchy cracker. These will disappear fast.

Rolled oats	1 cup	250 mL
All-purpose flour	1 cup	250 mL
Whole wheat flour	1 cup	250 mL
Granulated sugar	¼ cup	60 mL
Baking soda	½ tsp.	2 mL
Butter or hard margarine, melted	½ cup	125 mL
Sour cream or yogurt	½ cup	125 mL

Stir first 5 ingredients together in medium bowl.

Add butter and sour cream to flour mixture. Mix. Roll as thin as you can on lightly floured surface. Cut in strips 1 x 3 inch (2.5 x 7.5 cm) in size. Arrange on ungreased baking sheet. Prick with fork in several places. Bake in 350°F (175°C) oven for 10 to 12 minutes until golden. Makes 10½ dozen.

Pictured on page 89.

When the bald man was given a comb he said, "Thank you, I'll never part with it."

LAVOSH

Break in random-size pieces to enjoy with soup, as an appetizer or as a snack by itself. La-VAHSH is an Armenian flatbread.

All-purpose flour	2½ cups	625 mL
Granulated sugar	1 tsp.	5 mL
Salt	1 tsp.	5 mL
Water	⅔ cup	150 mL
Egg white (large)	1	1
Butter or hard margarine, melted	2 tbsp.	30 mL
Egg white (large), beaten	2 tbsp.	30 mL
Sesame seeds	2 tbsp.	30 mL

Stir flour, sugar and salt together in large bowl.

Add water, first egg white and melted butter. Mix well. Dough will be stiff. Divide dough into 10 balls. Roll ball on lightly floured surface until paper thin. Place on ungreased baking sheet.

Brush top with second egg white. Sprinkle with a few sesame seeds. Bake in 400°F (205°C) oven for about 10 to 12 minutes until browned. Repeat for remaining 9 balls. Makes 10.

Pictured on page 89.

FLATBREAD

Flat, dark and crunchy good.

All-purpose flour	2 cups	500 mL
Whole wheat flour	2 cups	500 mL
Natural bran (not cereal)	2 cups	500 mL
Granulated sugar	¼ cup	60 mL
Salt	1 tbsp.	15 mL
Baking powder	2 tsp.	10 mL
Baking soda	1 tsp.	5 mL
Hot water (not boiling)	1 cup	250 mL
Butter or hard margarine, cut up	¾ cup	175 mL
Buttermilk, fresh or reconstituted from powder	1 cup	250 mL

(continued on next page)

Measure first 7 ingredients into large bowl. Mix well.

Combine hot water and butter in small bowl. Stir until butter melts.

Add buttermilk to butter mixture. Stir. Pour over flour mixture. Stir lightly, just enough to moisten. Shape into about 22 balls the size of an egg. An ice cream scoop works well to measure ¼ cup (60 mL) dough. Roll each ball on lightly floured surface until paper thin using a lefse rolling pin if possible. Cook on ungreased lefse grill or frying pan at 400°F (205°C) to brown both sides, turning once. Put in 200°F (95°C) oven on paper towel-lined baking sheet to dry, about 4 to 5 minutes. Makes 22.

Pictured on page 89.

SWEDISH POCKETS

Very tasty. Cut in half and fill pockets with sliced tomatoes, cheese slices or cold meats. Or cut in wedges and eat as a snack.

Buttermilk, fresh or reconstituted from powder	2½ cups	625 mL
Butter or hard margarine	½ cup	125 mL
Salt	1 tbsp.	15 mL
Granulated sugar	1 tsp.	5 mL
Warm water	¼ cup	60 mL
Active dry yeast	2 x ¼ oz.	2 x 8 g
Rye flour	2 cups	500 mL
All-purpose flour	4½ cups	1.1 L

In the evening, scald buttermilk in saucepan. Remove from heat. Stir in butter and salt to melt butter. Cool to lukewarm.

Stir sugar in warm water in large bowl. Sprinkle yeast over top. Let stand 10 minutes. Stir to dissolve yeast. Add buttermilk mixture. Stir.

Add rye flour. Stir. Add remaining flour. Stir. Turn out onto floured surface. Knead 8 to 10 minutes, until smooth and elastic. Place in greased bowl, turning once to grease top. Cover with greased waxed paper and tea towel. Let stand overnight. In the morning shape into egg-size balls. Roll out each ball ¼ inch (6 mm) thick and 4 inches (10 cm) in diameter. Arrange on ungreased baking sheets. Bake in 400°F (205°C) oven for about 10 to 12 minutes until golden. Remove to racks to cool. Cover immediately with tea towel or place in paper bag to retain softness. Makes 36.

PIZZA

Crusts may be frozen after the first baking time. When pizza night arrives, thaw, add your toppings and finish baking.

All-purpose flour	**3 cups**	**750 mL**
Instant yeast	**1 x ¼ oz.**	**1 x 8 g**
Baking powder	**1 tbsp.**	**15 mL**
Granulated sugar	**1 tsp.**	**5 mL**
Salt	**¼ tsp.**	**1 mL**
Cooking oil	**6 tbsp.**	**100 mL**
Warm water	**1 cup**	**250 mL**

Measure first 5 ingredients into large bowl. Stir.

Add cooking oil and warm water. Mix well. Turn out onto floured surface. Knead 30 to 40 times until smooth and elastic. Grease 2, 12 inch (30 cm) pizza pans. Divide dough in half. Roll and stretch to fit pans. Bake in 425°F (220°C) oven for 15 to 20 minutes. Remove and add your favorite pizza sauce, toppings and cheese. Bake in 425°F (220°C) oven for another 8 to 10 minutes. Remove to racks. Let stand 5 minutes before serving. Makes 2 crusts.

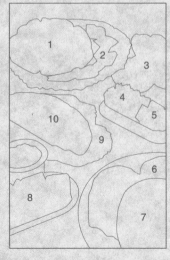

BANNOCK MODERN

Good nutty taste—much like a biscuit. Just a hint of sweetness.

All-purpose flour	2 cups	500 mL
Whole wheat flour	1 cup	250 mL
Baking powder	1½ tbsp.	25 mL
Brown sugar, packed	3 tbsp.	50 mL
Salt	1 tsp.	5 mL
Butter or hard margarine	¼ cup	60 mL
Milk (or water)	1¼ cups	300 mL

Measure first 5 ingredients into medium bowl. Cut in butter until crumbly.

Add milk. Mix until dough forms a soft ball. Roll or pat into ¾ to 1 inch (2 to 2.5 cm) thick round on greased baking sheet. Bake in 375°F (190°C) oven for about 40 minutes. To cook in greased frying pan, cook about 15 minutes per side. Makes 1 loaf.

Pictured on page 89.

EGG CRACKERS

Great for dipping in antipasto.

Large eggs	2	2
All-purpose flour	1¼ cups	300 mL
Baking powder	½ tsp.	2 mL
Salt	½ tsp.	2 mL

Beat eggs with spoon in medium bowl until blended. Mix in flour, baking powder and salt. Knead until smooth. Roll out ⅛ inch (3 mm) thick. Cut into squares. Place on ungreased baking sheet. Prick well with fork. Sprinkle lightly with salt or if you want more flavor, sprinkle with seasoned salt. Bake in 400°F (205°C) oven for about 5 minutes until golden brown. Makes 60 crackers.

Pictured on page 89.

BANANA LOAF

Gluten-free, this is a good substitute.

Large eggs	2	2
Granulated sugar	1/2 cup	125 mL
Cooking oil	1/4 cup	60 mL
Vanilla	1 tsp.	5 mL
Salt	1/2 tsp.	2 mL
Mashed banana	1 cup	250 mL
Milk	1/4 cup	60 mL
Brown rice flour	1 1/4 cups	300 mL
Potato starch	1/2 cup	125 mL
Tapioca flour	1/4 cup	60 mL
Cocoa	1 tsp.	5 mL
Gluten-free baking powder	1 tbsp.	15 mL
Baking soda	1/4 tsp.	1 mL

Beat eggs in medium bowl. Add next 6 ingredients. Beat. Mixture will be curdly.

Add remaining ingredients. Beat to mix. Turn into greased 9 x 5 x 3 inch (22 x 12 x 7 cm) loaf pan. Bake in 350°F (175°C) oven for about 45 minutes. An inserted wooden pick should come out clean. Makes 1 loaf.

YEASTY GLUTEN-FREE BREAD

Get the mild yeast flavor without kneading. Makes a dense loaf. Handy to freeze in packages of 2 slices or whatever quantities most likely to be used at a time.

Cooking oil	1/4 cup	60 mL
Granulated sugar	3 tbsp.	50 mL
Large eggs	2	2
Water	2 cups	500 mL
Brown rice flour	1 1/2 cups	375 mL
White rice flour	1 1/2 cups	375 mL
Buttermilk powder	1/3 cup	75 mL
Instant yeast	1 x 1/4 oz.	1 x 8 g
Xantham gum	3 1/2 tbsp.	17 mL
Salt	1 1/4 tsp.	6 mL
Butter or hard margarine, softened for brushing top	1 tsp.	5 mL

(continued on next page)

Combine first 4 ingredients in mixing bowl. Beat until blended.

Measure remaining 7 ingredients into separate bowl. Stir well. Add to mixing bowl. Beat on low for about 1 minute to mix. Turn into greased 8 x 4 x 3 inch (20 x 10 x 7 cm) loaf pan. Cover with greased waxed paper and let stand in oven with door closed and light on for about 30 minutes until dough reaches top edge of pan at sides. Bake in 375°F (190°C) oven for about 30 minutes. Turn out on rack to cool.

Brush warm top with butter. Makes 1 loaf.

CRANBERRY MUFFINS

Enjoy these with milk or coffee. Gluten-free.

Butter or hard margarine, softened	¼ cup	60 mL
Granulated sugar	⅓ cup	75 mL
Large eggs	2	2
Milk	1 cup	250 mL
Vanilla	1 tsp.	5 mL
Rice flour	2 cups	500 mL
Tapioca flour	¼ cup	60 mL
Gluten-free baking powder	1 tbsp.	15 mL
Baking soda	½ tsp.	2 mL
Salt	½ tsp.	2 mL
Halved cranberries, fresh or frozen	1 cup	250 mL

Cream butter and sugar in medium bowl. Beat in eggs 1 at a time. Add milk and vanilla. Stir. Mixture may be curdled.

Add next 5 ingredients. Beat.

Fold in cranberries. Fill greased muffin cups almost full. Bake in 350°F (175°C) oven for about 25 minutes. An inserted wooden pick should come out clean. Makes 12 muffins.

BLUEBERRY MUFFINS: Omit cranberries. Add 1 cup (250 mL) fresh or frozen blueberries.

GLUTEN-FREE BISCUITS

Quick and easy. Best eaten warm.

Rice flour	1 cup	225 mL
Potato starch	¾ cup	175 mL
Granulated sugar	2 tsp.	10 mL
Gluten-free baking powder	2 tsp.	10 mL
Salt	¼ tsp.	1 mL
Xantham gum (optional)	1 tsp.	5 mL
Butter or hard margarine	4 tbsp.	60 mL
Water or milk	⅔ cup	150 mL

Measure first 6 ingredients into medium bowl. Stir well. Cut or rub in butter until crumbly.

Add water. Stir until you can form a ball. Knead 6 to 8 times on rice-floured surface. Roll or pat a scant 1 inch (2.5 cm) thick. Cut into rounds with 2 inch (5 cm) biscuit cutter. Arrange on greased baking sheet. Bake in 350°F (175°C) oven for about 15 minutes. These do not brown much. Cool on rack. Makes 10 biscuits.

CURRANT BISCUITS: Add ¼ cup (60 mL) currants to dough.

CHEESE BISCUITS: Add ⅓ cup (75 mL) grated sharp Cheddar cheese to dough.

RICE MUFFINS

Gluten-free containing rice as well as rice flour.

Butter or hard margarine, softened	¼ cup	60 mL
Granulated sugar	2 tbsp.	30 mL
Large eggs	2	2
Milk	⅔ cup	150 mL
Vanilla	1 tsp.	5 mL
Cooked rice	1½ cups	375 mL
Rice flour, brown or white	1¼ cups	300 mL
Cornstarch	¾ cup	175 mL
Gluten-free baking powder	1 tbsp.	15 mL
Salt	½ tsp.	2 mL
Raisins or currants	½ cup	125 mL

(continued on next page)

Cream butter, sugar and 1 egg well in medium bowl. Beat in second egg. Add milk, vanilla and rice. Beat on low to mix.

Add rice flour, cornstarch, baking powder and salt. Beat on low to moisten.

Stir in raisins. Fill greased muffin cups almost full. Bake in 350°F (175°C) oven for 20 to 25 minutes until an inserted wooden pick comes out clean. Makes 12 muffins.

GLUTEN-FREE BREAD

Freeze part of the loaf and use as needed.

Cooking oil	1/3 cup	75 mL
Granulated sugar	2 tbsp.	30 mL
Large eggs	2	2
Milk	1 cup	250 mL
Lemon extract	1/2 tsp.	2 mL
Rice flour, brown or white	2 cups	500 mL
Potato starch	1 cup	250 mL
Gluten-free baking powder	4 tsp.	20 mL
Salt	1/2 tsp.	2 mL

Beat cooking oil, sugar and eggs together well in medium bowl. Add milk and lemon extract. Mix.

Add remaining ingredients. Beat on lowest speed to moisten. Turn into greased 9 x 5 x 3 inch (22 x 12 x 7 cm) loaf pan. Bake in 350°F (175°C) oven for 35 to 40 minutes until an inserted wooden pick comes out clean. Loaf doesn't brown much. Let stand in pan for 15 minutes. Carefully turn out onto rack to cool. Makes 1 loaf.

Paré Pointer

Take the lamp from the post. Now you have a lamp lighter.

CHEESY BEER BREAD

Serve warm, then toast leftovers. Looks great.

All-purpose flour	2¾ cups	625 mL
Baking powder	4 tsp.	20 mL
Granulated sugar	1 tbsp.	15 mL
Salt	½ tsp.	2 mL
Dry mustard powder	¼ tsp.	1 mL
Finely grated sharp Cheddar cheese	1 cup	250 mL
Beer, room temperature	12 oz.	341 mL
TOPPING		
Finely grated sharp Cheddar cheese	¼ cup	60 mL
Sesame seeds	1 tbsp.	15 mL

Stir first 6 ingredients together in medium bowl.

Add beer. Mix just to moisten. Turn into greased 9 x 5 x 3 inch (22 x 12 x 7 cm) loaf pan.

Topping: Sprinkle with cheese and sesame seeds. Bake in 350°F (175°C) oven for about 50 minutes. Serve warm. Makes 1 loaf.

Pictured on page 107.

No wonder time flies so fast. So many people are trying to kill it.

TOMATO HERB BREAD

A good spice combination. Easy and tasty.

All-purpose flour	3 cups	750 mL
Baking powder	4 tsp.	20 mL
Granulated sugar	1 tbsp.	15 mL
Whole oregano	½ tsp.	2 mL
Sweet basil	½ tsp.	2 mL
Salt	½ tsp.	2 mL
Tomato juice	1½ cups	375 mL
Butter or hard margarine, melted	¼ cup	60 mL

Combine first 6 ingredients in large bowl. Stir. Make a well in center.

Pour tomato juice and melted butter into well. Stir just to moisten. Turn into greased 9 x 5 x 3 inch (22 x 12 x 7 cm) loaf pan. Bake in 400°F (205°C) oven for 35 to 40 minutes. If loaf appears to be browning too much, lay a piece of foil over top. An inserted wooden pick should come out clean. Turn out onto rack to cool. Makes 1 loaf.

Pictured on page 107.

CORN MUFFINS

Very quick to prepare.

All-purpose flour	1¼ cups	300 mL
Cornmeal	⅔ cup	150 mL
Brown sugar, packed	½ cup	125 mL
Baking powder	1 tbsp.	15 mL
Ground cinnamon	1 tsp.	5 mL
Salt	½ tsp.	2 mL
Large egg	1	1
Cooking oil	¼ cup	60 mL
Plain yogurt (or milk)	1 cup	250 mL

Stir first 6 ingredients in medium bowl. Make a well.

Beat egg in separate bowl. Add cooking oil and yogurt. Beat. Pour into well. Mix just to moisten. Fill greased muffin cups almost full. Bake in 400°F (205°C) oven for 15 to 20 minutes. Let stand on rack 5 minutes before removing from pan. Makes 12 medium or 8 large muffins.

BOSTON BROWN BREAD

Historically eaten with Boston Baked Beans, this bread is wonderful with stew or even with coffee.

Cornmeal	2 cups	500 mL
All-purpose flour	1½ cups	375 mL
Salt	1 tsp.	5 mL
Buttermilk, fresh or reconstituted from powder	1 cup	250 mL
Mild molasses	1 cup	250 mL
Baking soda	1 tsp.	5 mL
Hot water	2 tsp.	10 mL
Buttermilk, fresh or reconstituted from powder	1 cup	250 mL

Measure cornmeal, flour and salt into large bowl. Stir.

Add first amount of buttermilk and molasses. Stir well.

Stir baking soda into hot water in small cup. Add to batter. Mix well.

Mix in remaining buttermilk. Turn into 2 greased 28 oz. (796 mL) cans, or 3 greased 19 oz. (540 mL) cans, or 1 greased 2 quart (2 L) casserole dish. Fill ⅔ full. Cover with foil. Secure foil with string. Place cans or dish in steamer with boiling water halfway up sides of containers. Cover steamer. Return water to a boil. Steam for 2 hours. Add more boiling water as needed to keep level up. Remove cans from water. Let stand 5 minutes before removing bread from cans. Serve sliced, either warm or cold. Makes 2 or 3 cans or one 2 quart (2 L) casserole.

Pictured on page 107.

Are garter snakes snappy?

This one will get rave reviews all around the lunch table. Onion topping is excellent.

TOPPING

Butter or hard margarine	2 tbsp.	30 mL
Medium onions, halved lengthwise and thinly sliced	2	2
Ground rosemary	1 tsp.	5 mL
Ground thyme, generous measure	1/4 tsp.	1 mL
Brown sugar, packed	1 tbsp.	15 mL

SCONE

All-purpose flour	3 cups	750 mL
Granulated sugar	1 tbsp.	15 mL
Baking powder	4 tsp.	20 mL
Baking soda	1/2 tsp.	2 mL
Salt	3/4 tsp.	4 mL
Whole oregano	1 tsp.	5 mL
Garlic powder	1/4 tsp.	1 mL
Sweet basil	1/4 tsp.	1 mL
Butter or hard margarine	6 tbsp.	100 mL
Large egg, beaten	1	1
Buttermilk, fresh or reconstituted from powder	1 cup	250 mL

Topping: Melt butter in frying pan. Add onion. Sauté until clear and soft. Remove from heat.

Add rosemary, thyme and brown sugar. Stir.

Scone: Measure first 8 ingredients into bowl. Cut in butter until crumbly.

Add beaten egg and buttermilk. Stir to make a soft dough. Turn out onto floured surface. Knead 6 times. Pat into 2 rounds about 1/2 inch (12 mm) thick on greased baking sheet. Score into wedges. Spread onion mixture over top. Bake in 425°F (220°C) oven for 20 to 25 minutes. Makes 2 scones, 12 wedges in total.

Pictured on page 107.

BISCUITS

Soft, flaky texture. Just right with jam or jelly or just butter.

All-purpose flour	**2 cups**	**500 mL**
Baking powder	**2 tsp.**	**10 mL**
Salt	**½ tsp.**	**2 mL**
Butter or hard margarine	**3 tbsp.**	**50 mL**
Baking soda	**½ tsp.**	**2 mL**
Buttermilk, fresh or reconstituted from powder	**1 cup**	**250 mL**

Place first 4 ingredients in medium bowl. Mix until crumbly.

Stir baking soda into buttermilk in separate bowl. Add to flour mixture. Mix until it forms a ball. Turn out onto floured surface. Knead 8 to 10 times. Roll or pat into a circle ½ to ¾ inch (1 to 2 cm) thick. Cut into 2 inch (5 cm) rounds. Place on greased cookie sheet 1 inch (2.5 cm) apart. Bake in 450°F (230°C) oven for 10 to 12 minutes. Place on racks to cool. Makes 16.

CHEESY ONION MUFFINS

Makes a nice breakfast muffin.

All-purpose flour	**2 cups**	**500 mL**
Envelope dry onion soup mix (stir before measuring)	**1 tbsp.**	**15 mL**
Granulated sugar	**1½ tbsp.**	**25 mL**
Baking powder	**2 tsp.**	**10 mL**
Baking soda	**½ tsp.**	**2 mL**
Grated sharp Cheddar cheese	**1 cup**	**250 mL**
Salt	**¼ tsp.**	**1 mL**
Large egg	**1**	**1**
Cooking oil	**⅓ cup**	**75 mL**
Milk	**1 cup**	**250 mL**

Measure first 7 ingredients into large bowl. Stir. Make a well in center.

Beat egg in separate bowl. Mix in cooking oil and milk. Stir. Pour into well. Stir to moisten. Fill greased muffin cups almost full. Bake in 400°F (205°C) oven for 15 to 20 minutes. Let stand on racks 5 minutes before removing from pan. Makes 12.

Pictured on page 107.

Flavored with almonds, these sweet rolls are just right with coffee or tea.

All-purpose flour	3³/₄ cups	925 mL
Granulated sugar	¹/₂ cup	125 mL
Baking powder	2 tbsp.	30 mL
Salt	1¹/₄ tsp.	6 mL
Butter or hard margarine	³/₄ cup	175 mL
Orange, cut and seeded, with rind	1	1
Large egg	1	1
Large eggs	2	2
Sour cream	1 cup	250 mL
Almond flavoring	1 tsp.	5 mL
Ground almonds	¹/₄ cup	60 mL
Chopped glazed cherries	²/₃ cup	150 mL
Finely chopped candied ginger (optional)	²/₃ cup	150 mL
FILLING		
Butter or hard margarine, softened	3 tbsp.	50 mL
Granulated sugar	¹/₄ cup	60 mL
Ground nutmeg	2 tsp.	10 mL

Glaze, see page 64
Cherries and almonds

Mix first 5 ingredients in large bowl until crumbly.

Place orange and 1 egg in blender. Process until orange is ground.

Add next 2 eggs, sour cream and flavoring. Process to mix.

Add almonds, cherries and ginger to flour mixture. Add blender contents. Stir to form a ball. Turn out onto floured surface. Knead 6 to 8 times. Roll into 24 x 14 inch (60 x 35 cm) rectangle.

Filling: Spread dough with butter.

Stir sugar and nutmeg together in small bowl. Sprinkle over butter. Roll up from long side like a jelly roll. Cut into 18 slices. Place on greased baking sheet. Bake in 375°F (190°C) oven for about 25 minutes.

Drizzle with Glaze. Sprinkle with cherries and more almonds if desired. Makes 18.

Pictured on page 107.

SOURDOUGH STARTER

Very easy—just takes patience. Once it is ready, use in buns, bread loaves, pizza crust and much more.

Active dry yeast	**1 x ¼ oz.**	**1 x 8 g**
Warm water	**½ cup**	**125 mL**
Warm water	**2 cups**	**500 mL**
All-purpose flour	**2 cups**	**500 mL**
Granulated sugar (or honey)	**1 tbsp.**	**15 mL**

Sprinkle yeast over first amount of warm water in medium bowl. Let stand 10 minutes. Stir to dissolve yeast.

Add second amount of warm water, flour and sugar. Beat until smooth. Cover with cheesecloth. Let stand at room temperature for several days, stirring 2 or 3 times each day. When ready, starter should have a sour smell with small bubbles gently rising to the surface. The process will take from 5 to 10 days. Turn into jar, cover and refrigerate.

To Replenish Starter: for each 1 cup (250 mL) of starter you use add ¾ cup (175 mL) all-purpose flour, ¾ cup (175 mL) water and 1 tsp. (5 mL) sugar (or honey). Stir well. Cover loosely. Allow starter to stand at room temperature until bubbly. This should be at least 1 day. Refrigerate.

To Feed Starter: If starter isn't used on a regular basis, stir in 1 tsp. (5 mL) sugar or honey every 10 days.

Have you ever seen a more plucky musician? She's a harp player.

The aroma is wonderful.

Granulated sugar	2 tsp.	10 mL
Warm water	1½ cups	375 mL
Active dry yeast	1 x ¼ oz.	1 x 8 g
All-purpose flour	2½ cups	625 mL
Salt	2 tsp.	10 mL
Baking soda	½ tsp.	2 mL
Sourdough starter, room temperature, see page 102	1 cup	250 mL
All-purpose flour, approximately	3 cups	750 mL
Butter or hard margarine, softened for brushing tops	2 tsp.	10 mL

Stir sugar in warm water in large bowl. Sprinkle yeast over top. Let stand 10 minutes. Stir to dissolve yeast.

Add next 4 ingredients. Mix well.

Work in enough remaining flour until dough pulls away from sides of bowl. Turn out onto floured surface. Knead 8 to 10 minutes until smooth and elastic. Place in greased bowl, turning once to grease top. Cover with tea towel. Let stand in oven with light on and door closed for 1 to 1½ hours until doubled in bulk. Punch dough down. Divide in half. Cover with tea towel. Let rest on counter for 10 minutes. Shape into round loaves. Place on greased baking sheet. Cover with tea towel. Let stand in oven with light on and door closed for about 1 hour until almost doubled in size. Bake in 400°F (205°C) oven for 30 to 35 minutes. Turn out onto racks to cool.

Brush warm tops with butter. Makes 2 loaves.

Just put your car in an oven if you would like to own a hot rod.

SOURDOUGH MUFFINS

Serve with butter or jam. Great for breakfast or lunch.

All-purpose flour	1¾ cups	425 mL
Granulated sugar	¼ cup	60 mL
Baking powder	2½ tsp.	12 mL
Salt	¾ tsp.	4 mL
Large egg, beaten	1	1
Milk	½ cup	125 mL
Cooking oil	⅓ cup	75 mL
Sourdough starter, room temperature, see page 102	½ cup	125 mL

Stir first 4 ingredients together in medium bowl. Make a well.

Add remaining ingredients to well. Stir to moisten. Fill greased muffin cups ¾ full. Bake in 400°F (205°C) oven for 15 minutes. An inserted wooden pick should come out clean. Makes 12.

SOURDOUGH BISCUITS

More "oomph" than a regular biscuit. Good 'sour' flavor.

All-purpose flour	1½ cups	375 mL
Baking powder	2 tsp.	10 mL
Baking soda	½ tsp.	2 mL
Salt	½ tsp.	2 mL
Cooking oil	⅓ cup	75 mL
Sourdough starter, room temperature, see page 102	1 cup	250 mL

Measure first 4 ingredients into medium bowl. Stir well.

Add cooking oil and sourdough starter. Stir to form a ball. Turn out onto floured surface. Roll or pat ¾ inch (2 cm) thick. Cut into 2 inch (5 cm) rounds. Arrange on ungreased baking sheet. Bake in 425°F (220°C) oven for about 12 minutes. Makes 16.

Pictured on page 107.

SOURDOUGH PIZZA CRUST

Crispy but tender crust. Sour flavor is subtle. This will become a favorite!

Sourdough starter, room temperature, see page 102	½ cup	125 mL
Cooking oil	2 tbsp.	30 mL
All-purpose flour	½ cup	125 mL
Baking powder	1 tsp.	5 mL
Baking soda	⅛ tsp.	0.5 mL
Salt	⅛ tsp.	0.5 mL

Combine sourdough starter and cooking oil in medium bowl.

Mix next 4 ingredients in cup. Add to sourdough starter mixture. Stir well. Press into greased 12 inch (30 cm) pizza pan. Bake in 425°F (220°C) oven for 10 minutes. Remove from oven. Cool for a few minutes. Proceed to add toppings of your choice. Bake until cheese melts and has a touch of brown. Makes 1 crust.

SOURDOUGH CORN MUFFINS

For the sourdough lover.

All-purpose flour	1 cup	250 mL
Yellow cornmeal	1 cup	250 mL
Baking powder	2 tsp.	10 mL
Granulated sugar	1 tbsp.	15 mL
Salt	½ tsp.	2 mL
Baking soda	¼ tsp.	1 mL
Ground thyme	¼ tsp.	1 mL
Large egg, beaten	1	1
Milk	1 cup	250 mL
Cooking oil	¼ cup	60 mL
Sourdough starter, room temperature, see page 102	½ cup	125 mL

Stir first 7 ingredients together in medium bowl. Make a well.

Add remaining ingredients to well. Stir to moisten. Fill greased muffin cups ¾ full. Bake in 400°F (205°C) oven for 15 minutes. An inserted wooden pick should come out clean. Makes 12.

BEER BREAD

Easy and fast. A delight to toast.

Whole wheat flour	3 cups	675 mL
Baking powder	1 tsp.	5 mL
Baking soda	½ tsp.	2 mL
Salt	½ tsp.	2 mL
Mild molasses	2 tbsp.	30 mL
Beer, room temperature	12 oz.	341 mL
Butter or hard margarine, softened, for brushing top	1 tsp.	5 mL

Mix flour, baking powder, baking soda and salt together in large bowl.

Add molasses and beer. Stir to moisten. Turn out onto floured surface. Knead 1 minute. Put into greased 8 inch (20 cm) round cake pan. Cut lines with sharp knife ½ inch (12 mm) deep marking 6 to 12 wedges. Bake in 325°F (160°C) oven for 40 to 50 minutes until bread cooks away from side of pan. Turn out onto rack to cool.

Brush warm top with butter. Makes 1 loaf.

Pictured on cover.

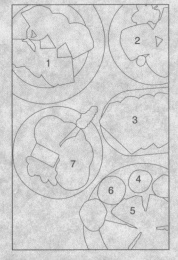

This light brown loaf contains rye flour and whole wheat flour. A bit of sweetness comes from the puréed raisins.

Milk, scalded and cooled to lukewarm	**2 cups**	**500 mL**
Brown sugar, packed	**²/₃ cup**	**150 mL**
Cooking oil	**¹/₃ cup**	**75 mL**
Raisins	**¹/₃ cup**	**75 mL**
Granulated sugar	**2 tsp.**	**10 mL**
Warm water	**½ cup**	**125 mL**
Active dry yeast	**2 × ¼ oz.**	**2 × 8 g**
All-purpose flour	**2½ cups**	**625 mL**
Salt	**1½ tsp.**	**7 mL**
Rye flour	**1½ cups**	**375 mL**
Whole wheat flour	**2¾ cups**	**685 mL**
Cornmeal		
Milk, for brushing tops	**1 tbsp.**	**15 mL**

Place first 4 ingredients in blender. Process until smooth.

Stir granulated sugar in warm water in small bowl. Sprinkle yeast over top. Let stand 10 minutes. Stir to dissolve yeast.

Measure all-purpose flour and salt into large bowl. Add blender mixture and yeast mixture. Beat for 2 minutes.

Mix in rye flour then work in whole wheat flour. Turn out onto floured surface. Knead 8 to 10 minutes until smooth and elastic. Place in greased bowl, turning once to grease top. Cover with tea towel. Let stand in oven with light on and door closed for about 1½ hours until doubled in bulk. Punch dough down. Divide into 4 equal portions. Shape into 4 round loaves.

Sprinkle 2 baking sheets with cornmeal. Arrange 2 loaves on each sheet. Cover with tea towel. Let stand in oven with light on and door closed about 45 minutes until doubled in size.

Brush tops with milk. Bake in 375°F (190°C) oven for about 35 minutes until browned nicely. Turn out onto racks to cool. Makes 4 small loaves.

Variation: Make slashes, ¼ inch (6 mm) deep on tops before baking.

Pictured on page 143.

ITALIAN BREAD

Contains straht-CHEE-noh cheese. Cream cheese may be substituted.
Also contains pro-SHOO-toh.

Granulated sugar	1 tsp.	5 mL
Warm milk	¼ cup	60 mL
Active dry yeast	1 x ¼ oz.	1 x 8 g
Stracchino cheese (or cream cheese), softened	4 oz.	125 g
Large eggs	3	3
Olive oil (or cooking oil)	3 tbsp.	50 mL
Grated Romano cheese	½ cup	125 mL
Chopped prosciutto (or cooked ham)	1½ cups	375 mL
Pepper	¼ tsp.	1 mL
All-purpose flour, approximately	2⅔ cups	650 mL
Milk, for brushing top	2 tsp.	10 mL

Stir sugar in warm milk in small bowl. Sprinkle yeast over top. Let stand 10 minutes. Stir to dissolve yeast.

Beat stracchino cheese and eggs in large bowl. Mix in olive oil and Romano cheese. Add prosciutto and pepper. Stir. Add yeast mixture. Stir.

Work in enough flour until dough pulls away from sides of bowl. Turn out onto floured surface. Knead 8 to 10 minutes until smooth and elastic. Place in greased bowl, turning once to grease top. Cover with tea towel. Let stand in oven with light on and door closed for 1 to 1½ hours until doubled in bulk. Punch dough down. Place in greased 1½ quart (1.5 L) casserole dish. Cover with tea towel. Let stand in oven with light on and door closed about 45 minutes until doubled in size.

Brush top with milk. Bake in 375°F (190°C) oven for about 35 minutes. Turn out onto rack to cool. Makes 1 loaf.

Pictured on page 125.

A wonderful aroma to this big round loaf.

Granulated sugar	1 tsp.	5 mL
Warm water	½ cup	125 mL
Active dry yeast	1 × ¼ oz.	1 × 8 g
All-purpose flour	1 cup	250 mL
Granulated sugar	1 tbsp.	15 mL
Onion flakes	2 tbsp.	30 mL
Dill weed	2 tsp.	10 mL
Salt	1 tsp.	5 mL
Baking soda	¼ tsp.	1 mL
Cottage cheese	1 cup	250 mL
Butter or hard margarine	2 tbsp.	30 mL
Large egg	1	1
All-purpose flour	1¾ cups	425 mL

Stir first amount of sugar in warm water in small bowl. Sprinkle yeast over top. Let stand 10 minutes. Stir to dissolve yeast.

Measure next 6 ingredients into large bowl. Add yeast mixture. Beat on low to moisten. Beat on high 1 minute.

Place cottage cheese, butter and egg in saucepan. Beat together with fork. Heat and stir just until warm. Add to contents in large bowl. Beat 3 minutes.

Add remaining flour. Stir to moisten. Turn out onto floured surface. Knead for about 5 minutes. Place in greased bowl, turning once to grease top. Cover with tea towel. Let stand in oven with light on and door closed for 40 to 50 minutes until doubled in bulk. Punch dough down. Shape into round loaf. Place in greased 1½ quart (1.5 L) casserole or greased 9 x 5 x 3 inch (22 x 12 x 7 cm) loaf pan. Cover with tea towel. Let stand in oven with light on and door closed about 30 minutes until doubled in size. Bake in 375°F (190°C) oven for about 30 minutes. Turn out onto rack to cool. Makes 1 loaf.

Paré Pointer

A sick wasp goes to the Waspital.

WATER BREAD

An all-occasion bread. Soft and moist.

All-purpose flour	5 cups	1.25 L
Salt	1 tbsp.	15 mL
Granulated sugar	2½ tbsp.	40 mL
Instant yeast	1 x ¼ oz.	1 x 8 g
Warm water	4 cups	1 L
Cooking oil	¼ cup	60 mL
All-purpose flour, approximately	6 cups	1.5 L
Butter or hard margarine, melted, for brushing tops	2 tsp.	10 mL

Combine first amount of flour, salt, sugar and yeast in large bowl. Stir and make a well.

Pour warm water and cooking oil into well. Stir to moisten. Cover with greased waxed paper and tea towel. Place in oven with light on and door closed for 10 minutes. Remove from oven.

Work in enough remaining flour until dough pulls away from sides of bowl. Turn out onto floured surface. Grease hands to handle the sticky dough. Knead 8 to 10 minutes until smooth and elastic. Place in greased bowl, turning once to grease top. Cover with tea towel. Let stand in oven with light on and door closed about 1¼ hours until doubled in bulk. Punch dough down. Divide into 4 portions. Shape into loaves. Place in 4 greased 9 x 5 x 3 inch (22 x 12 x 7 cm) loaf pans.

Cover with waxed paper and tea towel. Let stand in oven with light on and door closed about 45 minutes until doubled in size. Bake in 400°F (205°C) oven for 20 to 25 minutes. Turn out onto racks to cool.

Brush tops of hot loaves with melted butter. Makes 3 or 4 loaves.

OLD FASHIONED BREAD: Use warm water that has been drained from boiled potatoes instead of just plain warm water.

A moist, dense loaf. Good with soup.

Boiling water	2 cups	500 mL
Cracked wheat	2 cups	500 mL
Brown sugar, packed	1/2 cup	125 mL
Butter or hard margarine	3 tbsp.	50 mL
Salt	2 tsp.	10 mL
Granulated sugar	2 tsp.	10 mL
Warm water	1/2 cup	125 mL
Active dry yeast	2 x 1/4 oz.	2 x 8 g
Whole wheat flour	2 cups	500 mL
All-purpose flour, approximately	3 cups	750 mL
Butter or hard margarine, softened, for brushing tops	2 tsp.	10 mL

Combine first 5 ingredients in large bowl. Stir well. Cool to lukewarm.

Stir granulated sugar into warm water in small bowl. Sprinkle yeast over top. Let stand 10 minutes. Stir to dissolve yeast. Add to large bowl. Stir.

Add whole wheat flour. Beat until smooth.

Work in enough all-purpose flour until dough pulls away from sides of bowl. Turn out onto floured surface. Knead 8 to 10 minutes until smooth and elastic. Place in greased bowl, turning once to grease top. Cover with tea towel. Let stand in oven with light on and door closed for about 1½ hours until doubled in bulk. Punch dough down. Divide in half. Place in 2 greased 9 x 5 x 3 inch (22 x 12 x 7 cm) loaf pans. Cover with tea towel. Let stand in oven with light on and door closed for about 45 minutes until doubled in size. Bake in 350°F (175°C) oven for about 30 minutes. Turn out onto racks to cool.

Brush warm tops with butter. Makes 2 loaves.

Some people have hearts of gold. Yellow and hard.

BLACK BREAD

Delicious dark round loaves. Quite a fine texture.

Rye flour	3½ cups	875 mL
All bran cereal (100% bran)	¾ cup	175 mL
Cocoa	¼ cup	60 mL
Salt	2 tsp.	10 mL
Caraway seeds (optional)	1 tsp.	5 mL
Butter or hard margarine, softened	¼ cup	60 mL
Instant coffee granules	1 tbsp.	15 mL
Dark cooking molasses	⅓ cup	75 mL
Fennel seeds	½ tsp.	2 mL
Onion powder	1 tsp.	5 mL
Warm water	2¼ cups	560 mL
Granulated sugar	1 tsp.	5 mL
Warm water	¼ cup	60 mL
Active dry yeast	2 × ¼ oz.	2 × 8 g
All-purpose flour	3½ cups	875 mL

Measure first 11 ingredients into large bowl. Beat on low to moisten.

Stir sugar into second amount of warm water in small bowl. Sprinkle yeast over top. Let stand 10 minutes. Stir to dissolve yeast. Add to contents in large bowl. Beat on low to moisten. Beat on high until smooth.

Work in enough remaining flour until dough pulls away from sides of bowl. Turn out onto floured surface. Knead 8 to 10 minutes until smooth and elastic. Place in greased bowl, turning once to grease top. Cover with tea towel. Let stand in oven with light on and door closed for 45 to 60 minutes until dough is almost doubled in bulk. Punch dough down. Divide into 2 equal portions. Shape into round loaves and put in 2 greased 8 inch (20 cm) round cake layer pans. Flatten slightly. Cover with tea towel. Let stand in oven with light on and door closed for 30 to 45 minutes until almost doubled in size. Slash tops of loaves with sharp knife. Make about 3 slashes per loaf. Bake in 375°F (190°C) oven for 35 to 40 minutes. Loaves should sound hollow when tapped. Turn out onto racks to cool. Makes 2 loaves.

A soft, yellow, moist loaf with a mild orange flavor. It looks and tastes wonderful.

Granulated sugar	**2 tsp.**	**10 mL**
Warm water	**½ cup**	**125 mL**
Active dry yeast	**2 x ¼ oz.**	**2 x 8 g**
Large eggs	**2**	**2**
Granulated sugar	**⅓ cup**	**75 mL**
Salt	**2 tsp.**	**10 mL**
Butter or hard margarine, softened	**¼ cup**	**60 mL**
Grated orange rind	**2 tbsp.**	**30 mL**
Prepared orange juice, warmed	**1 cup**	**250 mL**
All-purpose flour	**2½ cups**	**625 mL**
All-purpose flour, approximately	**2¾ cups**	**675 mL**
Butter or hard margarine, melted, for brushing tops	**1 tbsp.**	**15 mL**

Stir first amount of sugar into warm water in small bowl. Sprinkle yeast over top. Let stand 10 minutes. Stir to dissolve yeast.

Beat eggs in large bowl. Add second amount of sugar, salt and butter. Beat. Add yeast mixture. Stir.

Add orange rind to egg mixture. Add orange juice and first amount of flour. Beat on medium until smooth.

Work in enough remaining flour until dough pulls away from sides of bowl. Turn out onto floured surface. Knead 8 to 10 minutes until smooth and elastic. Place in greased bowl, turning once to grease top. Cover with tea towel. Let stand in oven with light on and door closed for about 1½ hours until doubled in bulk. Punch dough down. Divide in half. Shape into loaves. Place in 2 greased 9 x 5 x 3 inch (22 x 12 x 7 cm) loaf pans. Cover with tea towel. Let stand in oven with light on and door closed about 1 hour until doubled in size. Bake in 400°F (205°C) oven for about 35 minutes. Turn out onto racks to cool.

Brush warm tops with butter. Makes 2 loaves.

CHALLAH

This KHAH-lah (or HAH-lah) is sometimes a four-strand braid. Three strands are easier. A pretty loaf.

Granulated sugar	1 tsp.	5 mL
Warm water	½ cup	125 mL
Active dry yeast	2 × ¼ oz.	2 × 8 g
Butter or hard margarine	3 tbsp.	50 mL
Milk, scalded	½ cup	125 mL
Granulated sugar	2 tbsp.	30 mL
Salt	2 tsp.	10 mL
Large eggs	3	3
All-purpose flour	2 cups	500 mL
All-purpose flour	3 cups	750 mL
TOPPING		
Large egg	1	1
Water	1 tbsp.	15 mL

Stir sugar and warm water together in small bowl. Sprinkle yeast over top. Let stand 10 minutes. Stir to dissolve yeast.

Add butter to milk in large bowl. Stir to melt butter. Cool to lukewarm.

Add second amount of sugar, salt and eggs. Add yeast mixture. Beat on low to mix.

Add first amount of flour. Beat on low to moisten. Beat on high until smooth.

Add remaining flour. Turn out onto floured surface. Knead 5 to 10 minutes until smooth and elastic. Place dough in greased bowl, turning once to grease top. Cover with tea towel. Let stand in oven with light on and door closed for about 1¼ hours until doubled in bulk. Punch dough down. Divide dough into 3 equal portions for 1 loaf or into 6 portions for 2 loaves. Roll each portion to make 26 inch (65 cm) rope. Lay ropes side by side. Pinch the 3 ends together at one end. Braid strips. Pinch and tuck remaining 3 ends underneath. Place braided side up on greased baking sheet. Cover with tea towel. Let stand in oven with light on and door closed for about 35 minutes until almost doubled in size.

Topping: Combine egg and water in small bowl. Beat well with fork. Brush braid with egg wash. Bake in 400°F (205°C) oven for 25 to 30 minutes until golden brown. Makes 1 or 2 loaves.

Pictured on page 143.

PORTUGUESE SWEET BREAD

Creamy white and a large loaf. Contains eggs and mashed potato.

Milk	1 cup	250 mL
Butter or hard margarine	6 tbsp.	100 mL
Granulated sugar	¾ cup	175 mL
Granulated sugar	2 tsp.	10 mL
Warm water	½ cup	125 mL
Active dry yeast	2 × ¼ oz.	2 × 8 g
Large eggs	4	4
Salt	2 tsp.	10 mL
Cooked mashed potatoes	½ cup	125 mL
All-purpose flour, approximately	7½ cups	1.8 L
Butter or hard margarine, softened, for brushing tops	2 tsp.	10 mL

Heat and stir milk, butter and first amount of sugar in saucepan until milk is scalded. Cool to lukewarm.

Stir second amount of sugar into warm water in small bowl. Sprinkle yeast over top. Let stand 10 minutes. Stir to dissolve yeast.

Beat eggs in large bowl. Add salt and potato. Beat. Add milk mixture and yeast mixture. Stir.

Work in enough flour until dough pulls away from sides of bowl. Turn out onto floured surface. Knead 8 to 10 minutes until smooth and elastic. Place in greased bowl, turning once to grease top. Cover with tea towel. Let stand in oven with light on and door closed for 1 to 1½ hours until doubled in bulk. Punch dough down. Divide in half. Shape into 2 loaves. Place in 2 greased 9 inch (22 cm) pie pans. Cover with tea towel. Let stand in oven with light on and door closed about 30 minutes until doubled in size. Bake in 375°F (190°C) oven for 40 to 45 minutes. Turn out onto racks to cool.

Brush warm tops with butter. Makes 2 loaves.

FOCACCIA

This loaf knows no bounds. Use one of the listed toppings or make up your own. Foh-CAH-chee-ah is a fun loaf.

Granulated sugar	1 tsp.	5 mL
Warm water	¼ cup	60 mL
Active dry yeast	1 × ¼ oz.	1 × 8 g
All-purpose flour	3¼ cups	800 mL
Salt	1 tsp.	5 mL
Olive oil (or cooking oil)	2 tsp.	10 mL
Water	1 cup	250 mL

TOPPING 1

Small red onion, halved lengthwise and thinly sliced	1	1
Olive oil (or cooking oil)	2 tbsp.	30 mL
Coarse sea salt, sprinkle		

TOPPING 2

Small red onion, halved lengthwise and thinly sliced	1	1
Olive oil (or cooking oil)	2 tbsp.	30 mL
Brown sugar	1 tbsp.	15 mL
Coarse sea salt, sprinkle		

TOPPING 3

Olive oil (or cooking oil)	2 tbsp.	30 mL
Ground rosemary (may use more)	1 tsp.	5 mL
Dried thyme	¼ tsp.	1 mL
Ground sage	¼ tsp.	1 mL
Whole oregano	¼ tsp.	1 mL
Coarse sea salt, sprinkle		

TOPPING 4

Olive oil (or cooking oil)	2 tbsp.	30 mL
Sweet basil	¼ tsp.	1 mL
Garlic powder	¼ tsp.	1 mL
Ground pecans	1 tbsp.	15 mL
Coarse sea salt, sprinkle		

(continued on next page)

TOPPING 5

Olive oil (or cooking oil)	2 tbsp.	30 mL
Medium tomatoes, halved, seeded and diced	6	6
Granulated sugar	$\frac{1}{2}$-1 tsp.	2-5 mL
Sweet basil	$\frac{1}{4}$ tsp.	1 mL
Garlic powder	$\frac{1}{4}$ tsp.	1 mL
Coarse sea salt, sprinkle		

Stir sugar and warm water together in small bowl. Sprinkle yeast over top. Let stand 10 minutes. Stir to dissolve yeast.

Measure flour and salt into large bowl. Stir. Make a well in center. Add yeast mixture to well. Stir with spoon until mixed. Make a well once more.

Add olive oil and remaining water to well. Stir. Turn out onto floured surface. Knead for 8 to 10 minutes until smooth and elastic. Place in greased bowl, turning once to grease top. Cover with tea towel. Let stand in oven with light on and door closed for 1 to 1½ hours until doubled in bulk. Punch dough down. Place on greased baking sheet. Press or roll out to 12 inch (30 cm) circle. Makes 1 round flat loaf.

Topping 1: Soak onion in cold water for 30 minutes. Drain. Pat dry. Spread over top. Press onion down with fingers, making dents. Drizzle with olive oil allowing it to pool in dents. Sprinkle with salt. Let stand, uncovered, for 30 minutes. Bake in 400°F (205°C) oven for about 25 minutes. Serve warm or cold, cut in wedges.

Topping 2: Soak onion in cold water for 30 minutes. Drain. Pat dry. Spread over top. Press onion down with fingers, making dents. Drizzle with olive oil allowing it to pool in dents. Sprinkle with brown sugar and salt. Finish as in Topping 1.

Topping 3: Make dents with finger in surface. Drizzle with olive oil allowing it to pool in dents. Mix rosemary, thyme, sage and oregano. Sprinkle over top. Sprinkle with salt. Finish as in Topping 1.

Pictured on page 143.

Topping 4: Make dents with fingers in surface. Drizzle with olive oil allowing it to pool in dents. Mix basil, garlic powder and pecans. Sprinkle over top. Sprinkle with salt. Finish as in Topping 1.

Topping 5: Make dents with fingers in surface. Drizzle with olive oil allowing it to pool in dents. Spread tomato in large frying pan. Cook to reduce juice. Mix in sugar, basil and garlic. Spread over top. Sprinkle with salt. Finish as in Topping 1.

BRAN BREAD

Small loaves with a medium texture. Healthy.

Warm water	1½ cups	375 mL
Granulated sugar	¼ cup	60 mL
All bran cereal (100% bran)	2 cups	500 mL
Active dry yeast	2 x ¼ oz.	2 x 8 g
Large egg	1	1
Butter or hard margarine, softened	⅓ cup	75 mL
All-purpose flour	¾ cup	175 mL
Powdered milk	½ cup	125 mL
Salt	1½ tsp.	7 mL
All-purpose flour, approximately	3¼ cups	800 mL
Butter or hard margarine, softened, for brushing tops	2 tsp.	10 mL

Place first 4 ingredients in large bowl. Stir. Let stand 5 minutes.

Add egg, butter, first amount of flour, powdered milk and salt. Beat well.

Work in enough remaining flour until dough pulls away from sides of bowl. Dough will be sticky. Cover with greased waxed paper and tea towel. Let stand in oven with light on and door closed about 1 hour until doubled in bulk. Punch dough down. Divide in half. Shape into loaves and place in 2 greased 9 x 5 x 3 inch (22 x 12 x 7 cm) loaf pans. Cover with greased waxed paper and tea towel. Let stand in oven with light on and door closed about 45 minutes until doubled in size. Bake in 375°F (190°C) oven for about 40 minutes. Turn out onto racks to cool.

Brush warm tops with butter. Makes 2 loaves.

Naturally flies walk on ceilings. They'd get stepped on if they used the floor.

Dark round loaves. Good texture and excellent flavor.

Warm water	½ cup	125 mL
Granulated sugar	2 tbsp.	30 mL
Active dry yeast	3 × ¼ oz.	3 × 8 g
Mild molasses	⅓ cup	75 mL
Butter or hard margarine	2 tbsp.	30 mL
Salt	1 tbsp.	15 mL
Caraway seed (optional)	2 tbsp.	30 mL
Hot water	1¼ cups	300 mL
Rye flour	2½ cups	625 mL
Cocoa	¼ cup	60 mL
All purpose flour, approximately	3 cups	750 mL
Butter or hard margarine, softened, for brushing tops (see Note)	2 tsp.	10 mL

Stir warm water and sugar together in small bowl. Sprinkle yeast over top. Let stand 10 minutes. Stir to dissolve yeast.

Measure molasses, butter, salt, caraway seed and hot water in large bowl. Stir. Cool to lukewarm.

Add rye flour and cocoa. Beat to mix thoroughly. Add yeast mixture. Stir.

Add about ½ of the all-purpose flour. Mix. Work in enough remaining flour until dough pulls away from sides of bowl. Turn out onto floured surface. Knead 8 to 10 minutes until smooth and elastic. Place in greased bowl, turning once to grease top. Cover with tea towel. Let stand in oven with light on and door closed 45 to 60 minutes until doubled in bulk. Punch dough down. Divide dough into 2 equal portions. Shape into round balls. Place onto greased baking sheets. Cover with tea towel. Let stand in oven with light on and door closed 1 to 1½ hours until doubled in size. Bake in 375°F (190°C) oven for about 30 minutes. Turn out onto racks to cool.

Brush warm tops with butter. Makes 2 loaves.

Pictured on page 125.

Note: For a crispier crust, brush with water 2 or 3 times while baking. Omit brushing with butter after baking.

POTATO BREAD

Large loaves with a fine texture.

Medium potatoes, peeled and quartered	2	2
Water	2 cups	500 mL
Granulated sugar	1 tsp.	5 mL
Reserved warm potato water	½ cup	125 mL
Active dry yeast	1 x ¼ oz.	1 x 8 g
Large eggs	2	2
Milk, scalded and cooled to lukewarm	1¼ cups	300 mL
Butter or hard margarine	½ cup	125 mL
Granulated sugar	½ cup	125 mL
Salt	2 tsp.	10 mL
Reserved mashed potatoes	1 cup	250 mL
All-purpose flour	3 cups	750 mL
All-purpose flour, approximately	5 cups	1.25 L
Butter or hard margarine, melted, for brushing tops	2 tsp.	10 mL

Cook potatoes in water until tender. Drain. Reserve ½ cup (125 mL) water. Mash potatoes. Reserve 1 cup (250 mL) potatoes.

Stir first amount of sugar into reserved lukewarm potato water in small bowl. Sprinkle yeast over top. Let stand 10 minutes. Stir to dissolve yeast.

Beat eggs in large bowl until frothy. Add next 6 ingredients and yeast mixture. Beat on low to moisten. Beat on high until smooth.

Work in enough remaining flour until dough pulls away from sides of bowl. Turn out onto floured surface. Knead 8 to 10 minutes until smooth and elastic. Place in greased bowl, turning once to grease top. Cover with tea towel. Let stand in oven with light on and door closed for 1 to 1½ hours until doubled in bulk. Punch dough down. Shape into 2 loaves. Place in 2 greased 9 x 5 x 3 inch (22 x 12 x 7 cm) loaf pans.

Brush with melted butter. Cover with waxed paper and tea towel. Let stand in oven with light on and door closed 30 to 40 minutes until doubled in size. Bake in 375°F (190°C) oven for 30 to 40 minutes until browned. Loaves should sound hollow when tapped. Turn out onto racks to cool. Makes 2 loaves.

A bread with a long history from pioneer days.

Boiling water	2 cups	500 mL
Cornmeal	½ cup	125 mL
Butter or hard margarine	3 tbsp.	50 mL
Mild molasses	½ cup	125 mL
Salt	2 tsp.	10 mL
Warm water	½ cup	125 mL
Granulated sugar	1 tsp.	5 mL
Active dry yeast	1 × ¼ oz.	1 × 8 g
All-purpose flour	2 cups	500 mL
All-purpose flour, approximately	4½ cups	1.1 L
Cornmeal	1 tbsp.	15 mL
Butter or hard margarine, melted	2 tsp.	10 mL
Cornmeal	1 tbsp.	15 mL

Gradually stir boiling water into first amount of cornmeal in large bowl. Add butter, molasses and salt. Stir well. Set aside to cool to lukewarm.

Stir warm water and sugar together in small bowl. Sprinkle yeast over top. Let stand 10 minutes. Stir to dissolve yeast. Add to cornmeal mixture. Stir.

Add first amount of flour. Beat on low to moisten. Beat on medium about 2 minutes.

Work in enough remaining flour until dough pulls away from sides of bowl. Turn out onto floured surface. Knead 8 to 10 minutes until smooth and elastic. Place in greased bowl, turning once to grease top. Cover with tea towel. Let stand in oven with light on and door closed for 1 to 1½ hours until doubled in bulk. Turn out onto floured surface. Divide into 2 equal portions. Punch dough down. Shape into 2 loaves. Sprinkle bottoms of 2 greased 9 x 5 x 3 inch (22 x 12 x 7 cm) loaf pans with second amount of cornmeal. Cover with tea towel. Let stand in oven with light on and door closed for 30 to 45 minutes until doubled in size.

Gently brush tops with melted butter. Sprinkle with third amount of cornmeal. Bake in 375°F (190°C) oven for 30 to 45 minutes until bread sounds hollow when tapped on bottom of loaf. Turn out onto racks to cool. Makes 2 loaves.

Pictured on page 143.

PARMESAN CHEESE BREAD

It's just as easy to make two of these. It looks very attractive before and after slicing or if you wish to serve it hot, just pull apart.

Frozen bread dough	1	1
Butter or hard margarine	¼ cup	60 mL
Grated Parmesan cheese	½ cup	125 mL

Thaw covered dough at room temperature for 3 hours. Cut loaf into 12 equal pieces. Form into balls. Grease non-stick 9 x 5 x 3 inch (22 x 12 x 7 cm) loaf pan. If you don't have a non-stick pan, line pan with foil. Grease foil.

Melt butter in saucepan. Dip each ball of dough in butter. Roll in cheese. Place 8 balls in single layer in bottom of pan. Place remaining 4 balls down center. If there is any melted butter left, drizzle over top. Sprinkle any remaining cheese over top. Cover with greased waxed paper and tea towel. Let stand in oven with light on and door closed about 1 hour until doubled in size. Bake in 350°F (175°C) oven for about 30 minutes. Lay a piece of foil over loaf if it browns too fast. Turn out onto rack to cool. Makes 1 loaf.

Pictured on cover.

1. French Bread, page 128
2. Whole Wheat Bagels, page 69
3. Bagels, page 68
4. Italian Bread, page 110
5. Raisin Bread, page 130
6. Pumpernickel, page 121
7. Honey Cream Cheese, page 69

With an oatmeal topping it's easy to guess what kind of bread this is.

Rolled oats	1 cup	250 mL
Butter or hard margarine	3 tbsp.	50 mL
Mild molasses	¼ cup	60 mL
Boiling water	2 cups	500 mL
Warm water	¼ cup	60 mL
Granulated sugar	1 tsp.	5 mL
Active dry yeast	1 x ¼ oz.	1 x 8 g
Brown sugar, packed	⅓ cup	75 mL
Salt	2 tsp.	10 mL
All-purpose flour	2 cups	500 mL
All-purpose flour, approximately	4 cups	1 L
TOPPING		
Egg white (large)	1	1
Water	1 tbsp.	15 mL
Rolled oats	¼ cup	60 mL

Measure rolled oats into large bowl. Add butter and molasses. Pour boiling water over top. Stir. Cool to lukewarm.

Stir warm water and granulated sugar together in small bowl. Sprinkle yeast over top. Let stand 10 minutes. Stir to dissolve yeast. Add to warm rolled oat mixture.

Add brown sugar, salt and first amount of flour. Beat well.

Work in enough remaining flour until dough pulls away from sides of bowl. Turn out onto floured surface. Knead 8 to 10 minutes until smooth and elastic. Place in greased bowl, turning once to grease top. Cover with tea towel. Let stand in oven with light on and door closed for 1 to 1½ hours until doubled in bulk. Punch dough down. Divide into 2 equal portions. Shape into loaves. Place in 2 greased 9 x 5 x 3 inch (22 x 12 x 7 cm) loaf pans. Cover with tea towel. Let stand in oven with light on and door closed 20 to 40 minutes until doubled in size.

Topping: Beat egg white and water with fork in small bowl. Brush over tops of loaves.

Sprinkle with rolled oats using some or all, as desired. If you prefer not to use this topping, brush tops with softened butter after loaves are baked. Bake in 350°F (175°C) oven for 45 to 50 minutes. Turn out onto racks to cool. Makes 2 loaves.

Pictured on page 143.

FRENCH BREAD

Eat as is or use to make your favorite barbecue loaf. Best eaten fresh.

All-purpose flour	**2 cups**	**500 mL**
Salt	**2 tsp.**	**10 mL**
Active dry yeast	**2 × ¼ oz.**	**2 × 8 g**
Granulated sugar	**1 tbsp.**	**15 mL**
Warm water	**2 cups**	**500 mL**
All-purpose flour, approximately	**3 cups**	**750 mL**
Cornmeal, sprinkle		
Egg white (large)	**1**	**1**
Water	**1 tbsp.**	**15 mL**

Place first 4 ingredients in large bowl. Stir.

Add warm water. Beat on low to moisten. Beat on high for 3 minutes.

Work in enough remaining flour until dough pulls away from sides of bowl. Turn out onto floured surface. Knead 8 to 10 minutes until smooth and elastic. Place in greased bowl, turning once to grease top. Cover with tea towel. Let stand in oven with light on and door closed for 1 to 1¼ hours until doubled in bulk. Punch dough down. Divide into 2 equal portions.

Roll each portion into 12 x 15 inch (30 x 38 cm) rectangle on floured surface. Roll up from long side. Pinch to seal. Press ends to taper. Place seam side down on greased baking sheet that has been sprinkled with cornmeal.

Beat egg white and water together in small bowl with fork. Brush over loaves. Cover with tea towel. Let stand in oven with light on and door closed about 45 minutes until almost doubled in size. Make 3 diagonal cuts ⅛ inch (3 mm) deep across top of each loaf. Bake in 375°F (190°C) oven for 40 to 45 minutes. Turn out onto racks to cool. Makes 2 loaves.

Pictured on cover.

Variation: Although French Bread usually contains no fat, 1 tbsp. (15 mL) cooking oil may be added with the water to prevent it from drying out too fast.

BAGUETTES: Roll each portion into a long narrow loaf, up to the length your oven will hold. Slash before baking as for larger loaves. Bake at 375°F (190°C) for 40 to 45 minutes. Turn out onto racks to cool. Makes 2 loaves.

Pictured on cover and on page 125.

Quick and easy with a fine texture.

Warm water	**2 cups**	**500 mL**
Granulated sugar	**2 tbsp.**	**30 mL**
Butter or hard margarine	**2 tbsp.**	**30 mL**
Salt	**2 tsp.**	**10 mL**
Instant yeast	**1 x ¼ oz.**	**1 x 8 g**
All-purpose flour, approximately	**5½ cups**	**1.3 L**
Butter or hard margarine, softened, for brushing tops	**2 tsp.**	**10 mL**

Pour warm water into large bowl. Add sugar, butter and salt. Stir well to dissolve sugar and melt butter.

Sprinkle yeast over top. Stir to dissolve yeast.

Add about ½ the flour. Beat until smooth. Work in enough remaining flour until dough pulls away from sides of bowl. Turn out onto floured surface. Knead 8 to 10 minutes until smooth and elastic. Place in greased bowl, turning once to grease top. Cover with tea towel. Let stand in oven with light on and door closed for about 1 hour until doubled in bulk. Punch dough down. Divide dough in half. Shape into 2 loaves. Place in 2 greased 9 x 5 x 3 inch (22 x 12 x 7 cm) loaf pans. Cover with tea towel. Let stand in oven with light on and door closed for about 45 minutes until doubled in size. Bake in 400°F (205°C) oven for about 35 minutes. Turn out onto racks to cool.

Brush warm tops with second amount of butter. Makes 2 loaves.

RAISIN BREAD

A large loaf with lots of raisins. Cinnamon gives a real flavor boost.

Milk	**1¼ cups**	**300 mL**
Butter or hard margarine	**½ cup**	**125 mL**
Granulated sugar	**½ cup**	**125 mL**
Salt	**2 tsp.**	**10 mL**
Ground cinnamon	**2 tsp.**	**10 mL**
Granulated sugar	**2 tsp.**	**10 mL**
Warm water	**½ cup**	**125 mL**
Active dry yeast	**2 x ¼ oz.**	**2 x 8 g**
Large eggs, beaten	**3**	**3**
All-purpose flour	**3½ cups**	**875 mL**
Raisins, fresh and soft	**2 cups**	**500 mL**
All-purpose flour, approximately	**3½ cups**	**875 mL**
Butter or hard margarine, softened, for brushing tops	**2 tsp.**	**10 mL**

Scald milk in saucepan. Remove from heat.

Stir in next 4 ingredients. Stir to melt butter and dissolve sugar. Pour into large bowl.

Stir second amount of sugar into warm water in small bowl. Sprinkle yeast over top. Let stand 10 minutes. Stir to dissolve yeast. Add to large bowl. Stir.

Add eggs and first amount of flour. Beat on low to moisten. Beat on medium until smooth.

Add raisins. Mix. Work in enough remaining flour until dough pulls away from sides of bowl. Turn out onto floured surface. Knead 8 to 10 minutes until smooth and elastic. Dough may seem a bit sticky but handles well with greased hands. Place in greased bowl, turning once to grease top. Cover with tea towel. Let stand in oven with light on and door closed for about 1¼ hours until doubled in bulk. Punch dough down. Divide in half. Shape into loaves. Place in 2 greased 9 x 5 x 3 inch (22 x 12 x 7 cm) loaf pans. Cover with tea towel. Let stand in oven with light on and door closed for about 45 minutes until doubled in size. Bake in 350°F (175°C) oven for about 35 minutes. Turn out onto racks to cool.

Brush warm tops with butter. Makes 2 loaves.

Pictured on page 125.

So cheesy with a fine texture.

Milk	1½ cups	375 mL
Butter or hard margarine	2 tbsp.	30 mL
Granulated sugar	3 tbsp.	50 mL
Grated sharp Cheddar cheese	2 cups	500 mL
Salt	1½ tsp.	7 mL
Granulated sugar	2 tsp.	10 mL
Warm water	½ cup	125 mL
Active dry yeast	2 x ¼ oz.	2 x 8 g
All-purpose flour, approximately	6 cups	1.5 L
Butter or hard margarine, softened, for brushing tops	2 tsp.	10 mL

Scald milk in medium saucepan. Remove from heat.

Stir in next 4 ingredients. It is not a problem if cheese doesn't melt smooth. Cool to lukewarm.

Stir second amount of sugar into warm water in small bowl. Sprinkle yeast over top. Let stand 10 minutes. Stir to dissolve yeast. Add to cooled cheese mixture. Mix. Pour into large bowl.

Work in enough flour until dough pulls away from sides of bowl. Turn out onto floured surface. Knead 8 to 10 minutes until smooth and elastic. Place in greased bowl, turning once to grease top. Cover with tea towel. Let stand in oven with light on and door closed about 1 hour until doubled in bulk. Punch dough down. Divide into 2 equal portions. Shape 1 portion into loaf and place in greased 9 x 5 x 3 inch (22 x 12 x 7 cm) loaf pan. Divide second portion into 3 pieces. Roll each piece into 18 inch (45 cm) rope. Pinch 3 ends together. Braid ropes loosely, then pinch remaining 3 ends together. Place in greased 9 x 13 inch (22 x 33 cm) pan. Cover each pan with tea towel. Let stand in oven with light on and door closed about 30 minutes until doubled in size. Bake in 375°F (190°C) oven for 25 to 30 minutes. Turn out onto racks to cool.

Brush warm tops with butter. Makes 1 regular loaf and 1 braided loaf.

CHEESY HERB BREAD

Makes a large loaf. Spicy with a fine texture.

All-purpose flour	2 cups	500 mL
Instant yeast	1 × ¼ oz.	1 × 8 g
Chopped chives	2 tsp.	10 mL
Parsley flakes	2 tsp.	10 mL
Ground rosemary	¾ tsp.	4 mL
Ground marjoram	¾ tsp.	4 mL
Seasoned salt	¾ tsp.	4 mL
Onion powder	¼ tsp.	1 mL
Pepper	¼ tsp.	1 mL
Milk	1 cup	250 mL
Granulated sugar	2 tbsp.	30 mL
Salt	1½ tsp.	7 mL
Butter or hard margarine	¼ cup	60 mL
Large egg, beaten	1	1
Grated sharp Cheddar cheese	¾ cup	175 mL
All-purpose flour, approximately	1¾ cup	425 mL
Butter or hard margarine, softened, for brushing top	1 tsp.	5 mL

Measure first 9 ingredients into large bowl. Stir. Make a well.

Heat milk, sugar, salt and butter in small saucepan until quite warm. Pour into well. Mix. Add beaten egg and mix well.

Add cheese. Mix.

Work in enough remaining flour until dough pulls away from sides of bowl. Turn out onto floured surface. Knead 8 to 10 minutes until smooth and elastic. Place in greased bowl, turning once to grease top. Cover with tea towel. Let stand in oven with light on and door closed for 1 to 1½ hours until doubled in bulk. Punch dough down. Shape into loaf. Place in greased 9 x 5 x 3 inch (22 x 12 x 7 cm) loaf pan. Cover with tea towel. Let stand in oven with light on and door closed about 45 minutes until doubled in size. Bake in 375°F (190°C) oven for 30 to 35 minutes. Turn out onto rack to cool.

Brush warm top with butter. Makes 1 loaf.

Good wholesome flavor. One slice isn't enough.

All-purpose flour	1 cup	250 mL
Whole wheat flour	1 cup	250 mL
Rolled oats (not instant)	1/2 cup	125 mL
Yellow cornmeal	1/4 cup	60 mL
Natural bran (not cereal)	1/4 cup	60 mL
Wheat germ	1/4 cup	60 mL
Dark rye flour	1/4 cup	60 mL
Salt	2 tsp.	10 mL
Granulated sugar	1 tsp.	5 mL
Warm water	3/4 cup	175 mL
Active dry yeast	1 x 1/4 oz.	1 x 8 g
Very warm milk	2 1/4 cups	550 mL
Honey	3 tbsp.	50 mL
Dark cooking molasses	3 tbsp.	50 mL
Cooking oil	1/4 cup	60 mL
All-purpose flour, approximately	5 1/2 cups	1.3 L

Measure first 8 ingredients into large bowl. Stir.

Stir sugar and warm water together in small bowl. Sprinkle yeast over top. Let stand 10 minutes. Stir to dissolve yeast.

Combine next 4 ingredients in separate bowl. Stir. Add yeast mixture. Stir. Pour into dry ingredients. Beat until well mixed.

Stir in enough remaining flour until dough pulls away from sides of bowl. Knead 8 to 10 minutes. Place in greased bowl, turning once to grease top. Cover with tea towel. Let stand in oven with light on and door closed for about 1 1/4 hours until doubled in bulk. Punch dough down. Divide in half. Shape into loaves. Place in 2 greased 9 x 5 x 3 inch (22 x 12 x 7 cm) loaf pans. Cover with tea towel. Let stand in oven with oven light on and door closed about 45 minutes until doubled in size. Bake in 375°F (190°C) oven for 35 to 45 minutes. Turn out onto racks to cool. Makes 2 loaves.

Pictured on page 143.

WHITE BREAD

Any age loves fresh white bread.

Granulated sugar	1 tsp.	5 mL
Warm water	½ cup	125 mL
Active dry yeast	1 x ¼ oz.	1 x 8 g
Granulated sugar	2 tbsp.	30 mL
Butter or hard margarine, softened	2 tbsp.	30 mL
Salt	2 tsp.	10 mL
Scalded milk, cooled to lukewarm	2 cups	500 mL
All-purpose flour	2 cups	500 mL
All-purpose flour, approximately	4½ cups	1.1 L

Stir first amount of sugar into warm water in large bowl. Sprinkle yeast over top. Let stand 10 minutes. Stir to dissolve yeast.

Add next 5 ingredients. Beat on low to moisten. Beat on high until smooth.

Work in enough remaining flour until dough pulls away from sides of bowl. Turn out onto floured surface. Knead 8 to 10 minutes until smooth and elastic. Place in greased bowl, turning once to grease top. Cover with tea towel. Let stand in oven with light on and door closed for 1 to 1½ hours until doubled in bulk. Punch dough down. Divide into 2 equal portions. Shape into loaves. Place in 2 greased 9 x 5 x 3 inch (22 x 12 x 7 cm) loaf pans. Cover with tea towel. Let stand in oven with light on and door closed 35 to 45 minutes until doubled in size. Bake in 400°F (205°C) oven for about 30 minutes until browned. Loaves will sound hollow when tapped. Turn out onto racks to cool. Makes 2 loaves.

Insomniacs should sleep close to the edge of the bed and they will soon drop off.

A large, round, impressive loaf that is very tasty.

Milk	1 cup	250 mL
Butter or hard margarine	¼ cup	60 mL
Granulated sugar	¼ cup	60 mL
Salt	2 tsp.	10 mL
Granulated sugar	1 tsp.	5 mL
Warm water	½ cup	125 mL
Active dry yeast	1 x ¼ oz.	1 x 8 g
All-purpose flour	2 cups	500 mL
Whole oregano	1 tsp.	5 mL
Ground marjoram	½ tsp.	2 mL
Ground thyme	½ tsp.	2 mL
Garlic powder	¼ tsp.	1 mL
Instant minced onion	1 tbsp.	15 mL
All-purpose flour, approximately	2½ cups	625 mL
Butter or hard margarine, melted, for brushing top	2 tsp.	10 mL
Grated Parmesan cheese	1 tbsp.	15 mL

Heat and stir first 4 ingredients in saucepan until milk is scalded. Cool to lukewarm.

Stir second amount of sugar into warm water in small bowl. Sprinkle yeast over top. Let stand 10 minutes. Stir to dissolve yeast. Pour into large bowl. Add milk mixture.

Add first amount of flour and next 5 ingredients. Beat on low to moisten. Beat on medium until smooth.

Work in enough remaining flour until dough pulls away from sides of bowl. Turn out onto floured surface. Knead 8 to 10 minutes until smooth and elastic. Place in greased bowl, turning once to grease top. Cover with tea towel. Let stand in oven with light on and door closed 1 to 1½ hours until doubled in bulk. Punch dough down. Shape into round loaf. Place in greased 1½ quart (1.5 L) casserole dish. Cover with tea towel. Let stand in oven with light on and door closed for about 45 minutes until doubled in size.

Brush top with melted butter. Sprinkle with Parmesan cheese. Bake in 375°F (190°C) oven for about 30 minutes. Turn out onto rack to cool. Makes 1 loaf.

FRENCH ONION BREAD

Onion soup mix gives the flavor. Good with homemade soups or a barbeque.

Boiling water	1³/₄ cups	425 mL
Granulated sugar	3 tbsp.	50 mL
Butter or hard margarine	3 tbsp.	50 mL
Envelope dry onion soup mix	1 x 1¹/₄ oz.	1 x 42 g
Salt	2 tsp.	10 mL
Onion powder	¹/₄ tsp.	1 mL
Granulated sugar	2 tsp.	10 mL
Warm water	¹/₂ cup	125 mL
Active dry yeast	2 x ¹/₄ oz.	2 x 8 g
All-purpose flour, approximately	6 cups	1.5 L
Butter or hard margarine, softened, for brushing tops	2 tsp.	10 mL

Pour boiling water into large bowl. Add next 5 ingredients. Stir. Cool to lukewarm.

Stir second amount of sugar into warm water in small bowl. Sprinkle yeast over top. Let stand 10 minutes. Stir to dissolve yeast. Add to onion soup mixture. Stir.

Work in enough flour until dough pulls away from sides of bowl. Turn out onto floured surface. Knead 8 to 10 minutes until smooth and elastic. Place in greased bowl, turning once to grease top. Cover with tea towel. Let stand in oven with light on and door closed for about 1 hour until doubled in bulk. Punch dough down. Divide in half. Shape into loaves. Place in 2 greased 9 x 5 x 3 inch (22 x 12 x 7 cm) loaf pans. Cover with tea towel. Let stand in oven with light on and door closed for about 1 hour until doubled in size. Bake in 375°F (190°C) oven for 35 to 40 minutes. Turn out onto racks to cool.

Brush warm tops with butter. Makes 2 loaves.

Tops in flavor. And so different.

Millet (health food or oriental stores)	1/4 cup	60 mL
Boiling water	1 1/4 cups	300 mL
Granulated sugar	1 tbsp.	15 mL
Warm water	2 cups	500 mL
Active dry yeast	2 x 1/4 oz.	2 x 8 g
Reserved cooked millet	1/2 cup	125 mL
Whole wheat flour	2 1/2 cups	625 mL
Sliced and finely diced pepperoni, packed	3/4 cup	175 mL
Parsley flakes	1 tbsp.	15 mL
Black peppercorns, cracked (use bottom of water glass to crack on breadboard)	1 1/2 tsp.	7 mL
Salt	1 1/4 tsp.	6 mL
All-purpose flour, approximately	3 cups	750 mL
Egg white (large)	1	1
Water	1 tbsp.	15 mL

Cook millet in boiling water in small saucepan for about 10 minutes until tender. Drain. Measure and reserve 1/2 cup (125 mL).

Stir sugar into warm water in large bowl. Sprinkle yeast over top. Let stand 10 minutes. Stir to dissolve yeast.

Add next 6 ingredients. Stir well.

Stir in enough remaining flour until dough pulls away from sides of bowl. Turn out onto floured surface. Knead 8 to 10 minutes until smooth and elastic. Place in greased bowl, turning once to grease top. Cover with tea towel. Let stand in oven with light on and door closed for about 45 minutes until doubled in bulk. Punch dough down. Divide in half. Shape into loaves 12 to 14 inches (30 to 35 cm) in length. Place on greased baking sheet. Cover with tea towel. Let stand in oven with light on and door closed for about 30 minutes until almost doubled in size.

Beat egg white and water with fork in small bowl. Brush tops and sides of loaves. Bake in 400°F (205°C) oven for about 25 minutes. Makes 2 loaves.

SWEET CARDAMOM BREAD

When this is dressed up for tea it is a sure winner. Good cardamom flavor.

Milk	2 cups	500 mL
Butter or hard margarine	6 tbsp.	100 mL
Granulated sugar	¾ cup	175 mL
Salt	1½ tsp.	7 mL
Granulated sugar	2 tsp.	10 mL
Warm water	½ cup	125 mL
Active dry yeast	2 × ¼ oz.	2 × 8 g
Large eggs	3	3
Ground cardamom	1 tbsp.	15 mL
All-purpose flour, approximately	9 cups	2.2 L
GLAZE		
Icing (confectioner's) sugar	⅔ cup	150 mL
Water	2-3 tsp.	10-15 mL
Glazed cherries, quartered	⅓ cup	75 mL
Finely chopped walnuts or pecans	½ cup	125 mL

Scald milk in saucepan. Remove from heat.

Add butter, first amount of sugar and salt. Stir to melt butter and dissolve sugar and salt. Cool to lukewarm.

Stir second amount of sugar in warm water in small bowl. Sprinkle yeast over top. Let stand 10 minutes. Stir to dissolve yeast.

Beat eggs in large bowl. Add cardamom. Add milk mixture and yeast mixture. Stir.

Work in enough flour until dough pulls away from sides of bowl. Turn out onto floured surface. Knead 8 to 10 minutes until smooth and elastic. Place in greased bowl, turning once to grease top. Cover with tea towel. Let stand in oven with light on and door closed about 1¾ hours until doubled in bulk. Punch dough down. Divide into 3 equal portions. Place in 3 greased 9 x 5 x 3 inch (22 x 12 x 7 cm) loaf pans. Cover with tea towel. Let stand in oven with light on and door closed for about 45 minutes until doubled in size. Bake in 350°F (175°C) oven for 40 to 45 minutes. Turn out onto racks to cool. Makes 3 loaves.

Glaze: Mix icing sugar and water in small bowl to make a barely pourable glaze. Drizzle over loaves using back and forth motion.

TACO CORNMEAL BREAD

An orange shade to this yummy loaf. Just right to eat with chili or even just with butter.

Milk	1½ cups	375 mL
Granulated sugar	2 tsp.	10 mL
Warm water	½ cup	125 mL
Active dry yeast	2 × ¼ oz.	2 × 8 g
Large eggs	2	2
Honey	½ cup	125 mL
Cooking oil	½ cup	125 mL
Salt	2 tsp.	10 mL
Taco seasoning mix	2 × 1½ oz.	2 × 40 g
Whole wheat flour	2 cups	500 mL
Cornmeal	1½ cups	375 mL
Whole wheat flour	1 cup	250 mL
All-purpose flour, approximately	3¾ cups	925 mL
Milk, for brushing tops	2 tsp.	10 mL

Scald milk in saucepan. Cool to lukewarm.

Stir sugar into warm water in small bowl. Sprinkle yeast over top. Let stand 10 minutes. Stir to dissolve yeast.

Beat eggs in large bowl. Add milk and yeast mixture. Add next 6 ingredients. Beat on low to moisten. Beat on high until smooth.

Work in second amount of whole wheat flour. Work in enough all-purpose flour until dough pulls away from sides of bowl. Turn out onto floured surface. Knead 8 to 10 minutes until smooth and elastic. Place in greased bowl, turning once to grease top. Cover with tea towel. Let stand in oven with light on and door closed for 1½ to 1¾ hours until doubled in bulk. Punch dough down. Divide into 2 equal portions. Shape into loaves. Place in 2 greased 9 x 5 x 3 inch (22 x 12 x 7 cm) loaf pans. Cover with tea towel. Let stand in oven with light on and door closed for about 45 minutes until doubled in size.

Brush tops with milk. Bake in 375°F (190°C) oven for about 30 minutes. Turn out onto racks to cool. Makes 2 loaves.

BEER AND RYE BREAD

A real sandwich bread.

Granulated sugar	1 tsp.	5 mL
Warm water	½ cup	125 mL
Active dry yeast	1 x ¼ oz.	1 x 8 g
Beer, room temperature	12 oz.	341 mL
Butter or hard margarine, melted	3 tbsp.	50 mL
Granulated sugar	1 tbsp.	15 mL
Salt	1½ tsp.	7 mL
Mild molasses	½ cup	125 mL
Large egg, beaten	1	1
All-purpose flour	4 cups	1 L
Rye flour, approximately	3 cups	750 mL
Milk	2 tsp.	10 mL

Stir first amount of sugar into warm water in small bowl. Sprinkle yeast over top. Let stand 10 minutes. Stir to dissolve yeast.

Measure next 7 ingredients into large bowl. Mix. Add yeast mixture. Stir well.

Work in enough rye flour until dough pulls away from sides of bowl. Turn out onto floured surface. Knead 8 to 10 minutes until smooth and elastic. Place in greased bowl, turning once to grease top. Cover with tea towel. Let stand in oven with light on and door closed for about 1¼ hours until doubled in bulk. Punch dough down. Shape into 2 round balls. Place on greased baking sheets. Slash tops with sharp knife. Cover with tea towel. Let stand in oven with light on and door closed for about 1 hour until doubled in size.

Brush tops with milk. Bake in 375°F (190°C) oven for 25 to 30 minutes. Makes 2, 8 inch (20 cm) round loaves.

Fairly dense in texture. A stick-to-the-ribs bread.

Hot water	4³/₄ cups	1.1 L
Butter or hard margarine	3 tbsp.	50 mL
Mild molasses	½ cup	125 mL
Natural bran (not cereal)	1½ cups	375 mL
Granulated sugar	⅓ cup	75 mL
Salt	2 tsp.	10 mL
Warm water	½ cup	125 mL
Granulated sugar	2 tsp.	10 mL
Active dry yeast	2 x ¼ oz.	2 x 8 g
All-purpose flour, approximately	14 cups	3.5 L

Stir hot water, butter and molasses together in large bowl until butter melts.

Add bran, first amount of sugar and salt. Stir well.

Stir warm water and second amount of sugar together in small bowl. Sprinkle yeast over top. Let stand 10 minutes. Stir to dissolve yeast. Add to bran mixture. Stir.

Work in enough flour until dough pulls away from sides of bowl. Turn out onto floured surface. Knead 8 to 10 minutes until smooth and elastic. Place in greased bowl, turning once to grease top. Cover with tea towel. Let stand in oven with light on and door closed about 1 hour until doubled in bulk. Punch dough down. Divide dough in 4. Shape each piece into loaf. Place in 4 greased 9 x 5 x 3 inch (22 x 12 x 7 cm) loaf pans. Cover with tea towel. Let stand in oven with light on and door closed about 1 hour until doubled in size. Bake in 375°F (190°C) oven for about 35 minutes. Turn out onto racks to cool. Makes 4 loaves.

Cats had to run for their lives in China during the cultural revolution. They didn't say "Mao" properly.

NO-KNEAD WHITE BREAD

Wonderfully soft and moist. So easy.

Granulated sugar	3 tbsp.	50 mL
Warm water	2 cups	500 mL
Active dry yeast	1 × ¼ oz.	1 × 8 g
Salt	2 tsp.	10 mL
Butter or hard margarine, softened	3 tbsp.	50 mL
Large egg	1	1
All-purpose flour, approximately	5⅓ cups	1.3 L
Butter or hard margarine, softened, for brushing tops	2 tsp.	10 mL

Stir sugar into warm water in large bowl. Sprinkle yeast over top. Let stand 10 minutes. Stir to dissolve yeast.

Add salt, first amount of butter, egg and ½ the flour. Beat on low to moisten. Beat on medium for 2 minutes until smooth. Work in enough remaining flour until dough pulls away from sides of bowl. Cover with greased waxed paper and tea towel. Let stand in oven with light on and door closed for about 1 hour until doubled in bulk. Work batter down. Divide into 2 greased 9 × 5 × 3 inch (22 × 12 × 7 cm) loaf pans. Cover with greased waxed paper and tea towel. Let stand in oven with light on and door closed for about 30 minutes until doubled in size. Bake in 350°F (175°C) oven for about 30 minutes. Turn out onto racks to cool.

Brush warm tops with second amount of butter. Makes 2 loaves.

Pictured on cover.

1. Anadama Bread, page 123
2. Focaccia, page 118
3. Oatmeal Bread, page 127
4. Challah, page 116
5. Prairie Bread, page 109
6. Five Grain Bread, page 133

NO-KNEAD HOVIS BREAD

This dark, solid loaf will remind you of a European bread. Slice very thin to serve.

Milk	2 cups	500 mL
Mild molasses	$^1/_3$ cup	75 mL
Butter or hard margarine	2 tbsp.	30 mL
Salt	2 tsp.	10 mL
Ground ginger	$^1/_4$ tsp.	1 mL
Gravy browner	$^1/_2$ tsp.	2 mL
Natural bran (not cereal)	1 cup	250 mL
Wheat germ	$^1/_2$ cup	125 mL
Whole wheat flour	$2^1/_2$ cups	625 mL
Cocoa	$^1/_4$ cup	60 mL
Instant yeast	2 × $^1/_4$ oz.	2 × 8 g
Whole wheat flour, approximately	2 cups	500 mL

Scald milk in large saucepan. Pour into large bowl.

Add molasses, butter, salt, ginger and gravy browner. Stir. Cool to lukewarm.

Add bran, wheat germ, first amount of whole wheat flour, cocoa and yeast. Mix.

Work in enough remaining flour until dough pulls away from sides of bowl. Place in greased bowl, turning once to grease top. Cover with greased waxed paper and tea towel. Let stand in oven with light on and door closed for about 1$^1/_2$ hours until doubled in bulk. Punch dough down. Divide in half. Shape into small loaves. Place in 2 greased 8 x 4 x 3 inch (20 x 10 x 7 cm) loaf pans. Cover with greased waxed paper and tea towel. Let stand in oven with light on and door closed for about 40 minutes until doubled in size. Bake in 375°F (190°C) oven for 30 to 35 minutes. Turn out onto racks to cool. Makes 2 loaves.

Pictured on cover.

Paré Pointer

If you have something round with a bad temper, you have a vicious circle.

100% WHOLE WHEAT BREAD

Good size loaf. Light brown. A dense loaf.

Whole wheat flour	4 cups	1 L
Active dry yeast	2 x ¼ oz.	2 x 8 g
Milk	3¼ cups	800 mL
Brown sugar, packed	½ cup	125 mL
Mild molasses	¼ cup	60 mL
Butter or hard margarine	¼ cup	60 mL
Salt	2 tsp.	10 mL
Whole wheat flour, approximately	4½ cups	1.1 L
Butter or hard margarine, softened, for brushing tops	2 tsp.	10 mL

Measure first amount of flour and yeast into large bowl. Stir.

Combine milk, brown sugar, molasses, butter and salt in saucepan. Heat and stir until warm. Add to yeast mixture. Beat on low to moisten. Beat on high for 3 minutes.

Work in enough remaining flour until dough pulls away from sides of bowl. Turn out onto floured surface. Knead 8 to 10 minutes until smooth and elastic. Place in greased bowl, turning once to grease top. Cover with tea towel. Let stand in oven with light on and door closed for about 1 hour until doubled in bulk. Punch dough down. Divide in half. Shape into loaves. Place in 2 greased 9 x 5 x 3 inch (22 x 12 x 7 cm) loaf pans. Cover with tea towel. Let stand in oven with light on and door closed for 30 to 40 minutes until doubled in size. Bake in 375°F (190°C) oven for about 35 minutes. Turn out onto racks to cool.

Brush warm tops with butter. Makes 2 loaves.

When liars die they lie still.

SHREDDED WHEAT BREAD

A good chance to eat your cereal in your toast. Medium brown, good textured bread.

Shredded wheat biscuits	3	3
Mild molasses	1/3 cup	75 mL
Butter or hard margarine	3 tbsp.	50 mL
Granulated sugar	1 tbsp.	15 mL
Boiling water	1¾ cups	425 mL
Warm water	½ cup	125 mL
Granulated sugar	2 tsp.	10 mL
Active dry yeast	2 x ¼ oz.	2 × 8 g
All-purpose flour	6 cups	1.5 L
Butter or hard margarine, softened, for brushing tops	2 tsp.	10 mL

Place shredded wheat, molasses, butter and first amount of sugar in large bowl. Pour boiling water over all. Cool to lukewarm.

Stir warm water and second amount of sugar together in small bowl. Sprinkle yeast over top. Let stand 10 minutes. Stir yeast mixture into lukewarm shredded wheat mixture.

Work in enough flour until dough pulls away from sides. Turn out onto floured surface. Knead 8 to 10 minutes until smooth and elastic. Place in greased bowl, turning once to grease top. Cover with tea towel. Let stand in oven with light on and door closed about 1½ hours until doubled in bulk. Punch dough down. Shape into 2 loaves. Place in 2 greased 9 x 5 x 3 inch (22 x 12 x 7 cm) loaf pans. Cover with tea towel. Let stand in oven with light on and door closed for about 35 minutes until doubled in size. Bake in 375°F (190°) oven for 30 to 35 minutes. Turn out onto racks to cool.

Brush warm tops with butter. Makes 2 loaves.

Paré Pointer

A mummy will go out with any girl he can dig up.

RYE BREAD

Dark and dense. A fine texture and a mild hint of molasses.

All-purpose flour	3 cups	750 mL
Active dry yeast	2 × ¼ oz.	2 × 8 g
Cocoa	⅓ cup	75 mL
Instant coffee granules	2 tsp.	10 mL
Water	2¼ cups	550 mL
Dark molasses (blackstrap)	½ cup	125 mL
Butter or hard margarine	2 tbsp.	30 mL
Granulated sugar	2 tbsp.	30 mL
Salt	1 tbsp.	15 mL
Rye flour, approximately	3¾ cups	925 mL
Butter or hard margarine, softened, for brushing tops	2 tsp.	10 mL

Measure first 4 ingredients into large bowl. Stir.

Combine water, molasses, butter, sugar and salt in saucepan. Heat and stir until butter melts and mixture is warm. Add to bowl. Beat on low to moisten. Beat on high for about 3 minutes until smooth.

Work in enough rye flour until dough pulls away from sides of bowl. Turn out onto floured surface. Knead 5 to 7 minutes until smooth and elastic. Cover with tea towel. Let stand in oven with light on and door closed for 20 minutes. Divide dough in half. Shape into loaves. Place in 2 greased 9 × 5 × 3 inch (22 × 12 × 7 cm) loaf pans. Cover with tea towel. Let stand in oven with light on and door closed for about 1 hour until doubled in size. Bake in 375°F (190°C) oven for about 30 minutes until loaf sounds hollow when tapped. Turn out onto racks to cool.

Brush warm tops with butter. Makes 2 loaves.

Variation: For caraway lovers add 1 tbsp. (15 mL) caraway seed along with all-purpose flour.

What do you mean, maybe? A bee born in May?

Makes a large loaf containing eggs and a small amount of cornmeal.

Granulated sugar	1 tsp.	5 mL
Warm water	¼ cup	60 mL
Active dry yeast	1 × ¼ oz.	1 × 8 g
Warm milk	1¾ cups	425 mL
Granulated sugar	⅓ cup	75 mL
Butter or hard margarine, softened	6 tbsp.	100 mL
Salt	2 tsp.	10 mL
Large eggs, beaten	2	2
Cornmeal	¼ cup	60 mL
All-purpose flour	3 cups	750 mL
All-purpose flour, approximately	4½ cups	1.1 L
Butter or hard margarine, softened, for brushing tops	2 tsp.	10 mL

Stir first amount of sugar into warm water in small bowl. Sprinkle yeast over top. Let stand 10 minutes. Stir to dissolve yeast.

Combine next 7 ingredients in large bowl. Beat to moisten. Add yeast mixture. Beat until smooth.

Work in enough remaining flour until dough pulls away from sides of bowl. Turn out onto floured surface. Knead 8 to 10 minutes until smooth and elastic. Place in greased bowl, turning once to grease top. Cover with tea towel. Let stand in oven with light on and door closed for about 1½ hours until doubled in bulk. Punch dough down. Shape into 2 loaves. Place in 2 greased 9 × 5 × 3 inch (22 × 12 × 7 cm) loaf pans. Cover with tea towel. Let stand in oven with light on and door closed about 30 minutes until doubled in size. Bake in 375°F (190°C) oven for 35 to 40 minutes. Turn out onto racks to cool.

Brush warm tops with butter. Makes 2 loaves.

Paré Pointer

That couple is like the Amazon jungle. A bit dense.

EGG BREAD

Make these braids small or large. A fine texture with a crunchy crust.

Milk	1 cup	250 mL
Butter or hard margarine	$\frac{1}{4}$ cup	60 mL
Granulated sugar	$\frac{1}{3}$ cup	75 mL
Salt	2 tsp.	10 mL
Warm water	$\frac{1}{2}$ cup	125 mL
Granulated sugar	2 tsp.	10 mL
Active dry yeast	$2 \times \frac{1}{4}$ oz.	2×8 g
Large eggs, beaten well	2	2
All-purpose flour, approximately	$6\frac{1}{4}$ cups	1.6 L
Butter or hard margarine, softened, for brushing tops	1 tbsp.	15 mL

Scald milk in saucepan.

Put first amount of butter, first amount of sugar and salt into large bowl. Pour hot milk over top. Stir to melt butter. Cool to lukewarm.

Stir warm water and second amount of sugar in small bowl. Sprinkle yeast over top. Let stand 10 minutes. Stir to dissolve yeast. Add to lukewarm milk mixture.

Add beaten eggs. Work in enough flour until dough pulls away from sides of bowl. Place in greased bowl, turning once to grease top. Cover with tea towel. Let stand in oven with light on and door closed 1 to 1½ hours until doubled in bulk. Punch dough down. Divide into 2 portions. Cut each portion into 3 equal parts. Roll each part into 20 inch (50 cm) rope. Pinch 3 ends together. Braid on greased baking sheet. Repeat with remaining 3 ropes. Cover with tea towel. Let stand in oven with light on and door closed for about 45 minutes. Bake in 375°F (190°C) oven for about 30 minutes. Place on racks to cool.

Brush warm braids with second amount of butter. Makes 2 braids.

MEASUREMENT TABLES

Throughout this book measurements are given in Conventional and Metric measure. To compensate for differences between the two measurements due to rounding, a full metric measure is not always used. The cup used is the standard 8 fluid ounce. Temperature is given in degrees Fahrenheit and Celsius. Baking pan measurements are in inches and centimetres as well as quarts and litres. An exact metric conversion is given below as well as the working equivalent (Standard Measure).

OVEN TEMPERATURES

Fahrenheit (°F)	Celsius (°C)
175°	80°
200°	95°
225°	110°
250°	120°
275°	140°
300°	150°
325°	160°
350°	175°
375°	190°
400°	205°
425°	220°
450°	230°
475°	240°
500°	260°

SPOONS

Conventional Measure	Metric Exact Conversion Millilitre (mL)	Metric Standard Measure Millilitre (mL)
$1/8$ teaspoon (tsp.)	0.6 mL	0.5 mL
$1/4$ teaspoon (tsp.)	1.2 mL	1 mL
$1/2$ teaspoon (tsp.)	2.4 mL	2 mL
1 teaspoon (tsp.)	4.7 mL	5 mL
2 teaspoons (tsp.)	9.4 mL	10 mL
1 tablespoon (tbsp.)	14.2 mL	15 mL

CUPS

	Metric Exact Conversion	Metric Standard Measure
$1/4$ cup (4 tbsp.)	56.8 mL	50 mL
$1/3$ cup ($5^1/3$ tbsp.)	75.6 mL	75 mL
$1/2$ cup (8 tbsp.)	113.7 mL	125 mL
$2/3$ cup ($10^2/3$ tbsp.)	151.2 mL	150 mL
$3/4$ cup (12 tbsp.)	170.5 mL	175 mL
1 cup (16 tbsp.)	227.3 mL	250 mL
$4^1/2$ cups	1022.9 mL	1000 mL (1 L)

PANS

Conventional Inches	Metric Centimetres
8x8 inch	20x20 cm
9x9 inch	22x22 cm
9x13 inch	22x33 cm
10x15 inch	25x38 cm
11x17 inch	28x43 cm
8x2 inch round	20x5 cm
9x2 inch round	22x5 cm
10x$4^1/2$ inch tube	25x11 cm
8x4x3 inch loaf	20x10x7 cm
9x5x3 inch loaf	22x12x7 cm

DRY MEASUREMENTS

Conventional Measure Ounces (oz.)	Metric Exact Conversion Grams (g)	Metric Standard Measure Grams (g)
1 oz.	28.3 g	30 g
2 oz.	56.7 g	55 g
3 oz.	85.0 g	85 g
4 oz.	113.4 g	125 g
5 oz.	141.7 g	140 g
6 oz.	170.1 g	170 g
7 oz.	198.4 g	200 g
8 oz.	226.8 g	250 g
16 oz.	453.6 g	500 g
32 oz.	907.2 g	1000 g (1 kg)

CASSEROLES (Canada & Britain)

Standard Size Casserole	Exact Metric Measure
1 qt. (5 cups)	1.13 L
$1^1/2$ qts. ($7^1/2$ cups)	1.69 L
2 qts. (10 cups)	2.25 L
$2^1/2$ qts. ($12^1/2$ cups)	2.81 L
3 qts. (15 cups)	3.38 L
4 qts. (20 cups)	4.5 L
5 qts. (25 cups)	5.63 L

CASSEROLES (United States)

Standard Size Casserole	Exact Metric Measure
1 qt. (4 cups)	900 mL
$1^1/2$ qts. (6 cups)	1.35 L
2 qts. (8 cups)	1.8 L
$2^1/2$ qts. (10 cups)	2.25 L
3 qts. (12 cups)	2.7 L
4 qts. (16 cups)	3.6 L
5 qts. (20 cups)	4.5 L

INDEX

MAIL ORDER FORM

Deduct $5.00 for every $35.00 ordered

Save $5.00

COMPANY'S COMING SERIES

ENGLISH

Quantity		Quantity		Quantity	
	150 Delicious Squares		Vegetables		Microwave Cooking
	Casseroles		Main Courses		Preserves
	Muffins & More		Pasta		Light Casseroles
	Salads		Cakes		Chicken, Etc.
	Appetizers		Barbecues		Kids Cooking
	Desserts		Dinners of the World		Fish & Seafood
	Soups & Sandwiches		Lunches		Breads (NEW)
	Holiday Entertaining		Pies		Meatless Cooking (April '97) (NEW)
	Cookies		Light Recipes		

		NO. OF BOOKS	PRICE
FIRST BOOK: $12.99 + $3.00 shipping = **$15.99 each** x		=	$
ADDITIONAL BOOKS: $12.99 + $1.50 shipping = **$14.49 each** x		=	$

PINT SIZE BOOKS

Quantity		Quantity		Quantity	
	Finger Food		Buffets		Chocolate
	Party Planning		Baking Delights		

		NO. OF BOOKS	PRICE
FIRST BOOK: $4.99 + $2.00 shipping = **$6.99 each** x		=	$
ADDITIONAL BOOKS: $4.99 + $1.00 shipping = **$5.99 each** x		=	$

JEAN PARÉ LIVRES DE CUISINE

FRENCH

Quantity		Quantity		Quantity	
	150 délicieux carrés		Délices des fêtes		Les casseroles légères
	Les casseroles		Recettes légères		Poulet, etc.
	Muffins et plus		Les salades		La cuisine pour les enfants
	Les dîners		La cuisson au micro-ondes		Poissons et fruits de mer
	Les barbecues		Les pâtes		Les pains (août '96) (NEW)
	Les tartes		Les conserves		La cuisine sans viande (avril '97) (NEW)

		NO. OF BOOKS	PRICE
FIRST BOOK: $12.99 + $3.00 shipping = **$15.99 each** x		=	$
ADDITIONAL BOOKS: $12.99 + $1.50 shipping = **$14.49 each** x		=	$

TOTAL

- **MAKE CHEQUE OR MONEY ORDER PAYABLE TO:** *COMPANY'S COMING PUBLISHING LIMITED*
- **ORDERS OUTSIDE CANADA:** *Must be paid in U.S. funds by cheque or money order drawn on Canadian or U.S. bank.*
- *Prices subject to change without prior notice.*
- *Sorry, no C.O.D.'s*

TOTAL PRICE FOR ALL BOOKS	$
Less $5.00 for every $35.00 ordered −	$
SUBTOTAL	$
Canadian residents add G.S.T. +	$
TOTAL AMOUNT ENCLOSED	$

Please complete shipping address on reverse.

Gift Giving

- Let us help you with your gift giving!

- We will send cookbooks directly to the recipients of your choice if you give us their names and addresses.

- Be sure to specify the titles you wish to send to each person.

- If you would like to include your personal note or card, we will be pleased to enclose it with your gift order.

- Company's Coming Cookbooks make excellent gifts. Birthdays, bridal showers, Mother's Day, Father's Day, graduation or any occasion... collect them all!

Shipping address

Send the Company's Coming Cookbooks listed on the reverse side of this coupon, to:

Name:

Street:

City: Province/State:

Postal Code/Zip: Tel: (   )   —

COOKBOOKS

Company's Coming Publishing Limited
Box 8037, Station F
Edmonton, Alberta, Canada T6H 4N9
Tel: (403) 450-6223
Fax: (403) 450-1857

Sample Recipe from
Meatless Cooking

ZUCCHINI CUTLETS

So colorful with red and green showing throughout. A wonderful addition to a meal.

Finely grated carrot	½ cup	125 mL
Chopped onion	½ cup	125 mL
Chopped red pepper	¼ cup	60 mL
Chopped green pepper	¼ cup	60 mL
Fine soda cracker crumbs	2 cups	500 mL
All-purpose flour	¼ cup	60 mL
Baking powder	1 tsp.	5 mL
Salt	¾ tsp.	4 mL
Pepper	⅛ tsp.	0.5 mL
Grated zucchini, with peel	3 cups	750 mL
Large eggs, lightly beaten	2	2
Cooking oil	2 tbsp.	30 mL

Measure first 9 ingredients into bowl. Stir.

Mix in zucchini and eggs. Shape into cutlets (patties) using about ¼ cup (60 mL) for each.

Heat cooking oil in frying pan. Brown cutlets on both sides. Makes about 1 dozen.

Variation: For more protein add grated cheese.